#startupeverywhere

Startup Guide New York

EDITORIAL
Publisher: Sissel Hansen
Editor: Marissa van Uden
Proofreader: Ted Hermann
Contributing Editor: Charmaine Li
Staff Writers: Phineas Rueckert, Matthew Speiser, Cara Eisenpress, Charmaine Li
Contributing Writers: Emily Forsythe

PRODUCTION
Production Managers: Marcos Dinnerstein, Eglė Duleckytė
Researchers: Sean Ludwig, Emily Forsythe, Brian Frumberg, Shelley Pascual
Local Support: Gianluca Galletto, James Knowles

DESIGN & PHOTOGRAPHY
Designer: Ines Pedro
Photographers: Ryan Song, Anna Andersen

Additional photography by
Ryan Song, Anna Andersen, Joana Carvalho, Mayor's Office, UN Global Compact, The Muse (themuse.com), Ben Kelmer, Colleen Marie (colorsofcolleen.com), Craig Williston, Maria Jesus Verdugo, PencilWorks, Mikiko Kikuyama, Anthony Chatmon, Anders Birger, Domenica Gallinatti, David Yellen, Collision Conference, Alan Shapiro, Steven Duarte (stevenduarte.com), Columbia University, James Ewing (Courtesy of The New School), Lerer Hippeau, Brian Cohen, Ines Pedro, Hudson Yard (courtesy of Related-Oxford), WeWork and Unsplash.com

Illustrations by Joana Carvalho
Photo Editor: Daniela Carducci

SALES & DISTRIBUTION
Head of Sales: Marlene do Vale marlene@startupguide.com
Head of Community Growth: Eglė Duleckytė egle@startupguide.com
Head of Business Development: Anna Weissensteiner anna@startupguide.com
Head of Distribution: İrem Topçuoğlu irem@startupguide.com

Printed in Berlin, Germany by
Medialis-Offsetdruck GmbH
Heidelbergerstraße 65, 12435 Berlin

Published by Startup Guide World IVS
Kanonbådsvej 2, 1437 Copenhagen K

info@startupguide.com
Visit us: startupguide.com
@StartupGuideHQ

Worldwide distribution by Die Gestalten
Visit: gestalten.com

ISBN: 978-3-947624-06-5

STARTUP GUIDE NEW YORK

STARTUP GUIDE NEW YORK

In partnership with **Tech:NYC**

Proudly supported by

SAP next-**gen**

Sissel Hansen / Startup Guide

New York has long been known as one of the most diverse and creative cities in the world, but recently it's been growing a reputation for something else: in the past couple of years especially, the city's startup community has gradually come into its own and made a name for itself.

According to *Bloomberg*, companies in the New York metro area landed $13.3 billion in 2017, which is 70 percent higher than in 2015. No doubt, a big part of this shift is thanks to WeWork's massive funding round that year. Although New York was still in second place in terms of deal value across the US in 2017 (one spot below the San Francisco Bay Area), the gap seems to be narrowing. Not only that, according to a study by our local community partner Tech:NYC, the number of tech jobs in New York has increased by 30 percent in the past decade.

What makes New York's startup scene stand out from the rest is its close proximity to a mix of established industries beyond tech, such as fashion, media, real estate, art and finance, to name a few. This means there's more cross-pollination of ideas from different realms, which creates startups of all stripes. Think crowdfunding platform Kickstarter, online art marketplace Artsy and wedding registry site Zola.

Perhaps this kind of diversity is also why the Big Apple is a better place for women entrepreneurs than other cities in America. According to a report by Dell that examines cities' abilities to attract and support women entrepreneurs around the world, it ranked as the number-one place for women entrepreneurs in 2017.

For these reasons, we're beyond excited to have our first Startup Guide book in the US feature the bustling city of New York, and we can hardly wait for you to flip through these pages and learn more about the people, places and programs shaping its startup scene.

Sissel Hansen
Founder and CEO of Startup Guide

Bill de Blasio / Mayor of New York City

Friends,

Welcome to New York City's vibrant startup scene. We hope you'll be inspired by the faces and spaces in this guide to be part of the next generation of digital innovation.

The case for New York City is simple: we are the global capital of commerce, culture and innovation. No city has a greater diversity of talent, of industries, and of collisions that fuel great ideas and companies.

My Administration is focused on developing the people, infrastructure and connections to nurture our tech ecosystem and give every New Yorker, in every zip code, the opportunity to succeed in it.

We launched the NYC Tech Talent Pipeline, a one-of-a-kind partnership with industry leaders to strengthen our tech workforce by equipping thousands of New Yorkers with the ready-to-work skills most in demand at tech firms. Our City's Chief Technology Officer is leading efforts to make broadband, smart city technologies and digital services accessible to every community. As part of our Equity and Excellence vision for our schools, we're making Computer Science for All a reality in every public school and doubling the number of Computer Science graduates from the City University of New York.

This is a city that takes leaps and is constantly reinventing itself. In the span of a decade, New York's tech sector has evolved from a cluster of pure-tech start-ups to an ecosystem of more than 350,000 workers permeating nearly every industry. We have fueled that transformation by proactively building out hundreds of thousands of square feet of step-out space for early-stage firms. We are pushing into new economic territory, with investments in Life Sciences and Cyber-Security to fuel new breakthroughs and launch New York City to the forefront of new industries.

New York City is where innovation meets the real world. We are building an inclusive tech community, one that reflects the extraordinary diversity of our city, opens up new career paths for New Yorkers, and partners with the public sector to tackle concrete challenges facing our city. Technology is vital to helping us not only be the most innovative, but the Fairest Big City in America.

We hope this guide will encourage you to come and be a part of it all.

Alicia Glen / NYC Deputy Mayor

Commerce, culture and innovation keep the New York City startup economy running – and it's that distinct energy that makes our city the world's favorite place to do business.

But we know it's not enough to be the world's favorite; we must also be the world's fairest. That's why we're proud to be a global leader for women in startups.

No other city has more female-founded firms, and a quarter of our city's tech founders are women. We're consistently ranked the top global city for women entrepreneurs. And there is nowhere in which women are making bigger strides than in our quickest-growing sector, tech.

This is not an accident: We've taken substantive steps to make sure that NYC's start-up scene is open and accessible to women. From taking action against pay discrimination, to awarding more than $1 billion in City contracts to minority and women business enterprises and making direct investments in women-founded firms through programs like WENYC, we're setting the standard for supporting women entrepreneurs and professionals. And with this year's launch of women.nyc, we've created a portal and a resource model that's already being replicated by cities across the country.

The startups flocking to NYC are creating countless new opportunities and new ways of doing business, but throughout these changes, one fundamental quality will remain: NYC will always be where women come to succeed.

Alicia Glen
NYC Deputy Mayor for Housing and Economic Development

Lise Kingo / Executive Director and CEO of the UN Global Compact

Welcome to New York, the beating heart of future business.

New York City was, in fact, a Dutch company before it became a city. Entrepreneurial spirit and high energy are embedded in every one of the city's breaths. New York City is home to a fast-growing, constructive and creative startup scene, and everybody is invited to join.

As the executive director and CEO of the UN Global Compact, the world's largest sustainability initiative, I rely on entrepreneurs to build new companies in accordance with the seventeen Global Goals. All 193 member states of the United Nations have adopted a fifteen-year plan for achieving a better future for all: to end extreme poverty, fight inequality and injustice, and protect our planet. At the heart of "Agenda 2030" are the seventeen sustainable development goals, which clearly define the world we want, apply to all nations, and leave no one behind. A crucial step was to acknowledge that this can only be done with the participation of business.

For ambitious new entrepreneurs, the most crucial strategy decision for your business will be to embed the Global Goals in your growth journey. Responsible business is good business, and few companies will succeed if our society is broken, which it will be if we don't work together to change the current trajectory.
We need to create 600 million new jobs in the coming years to avoid mass unemployment leading to poverty. Together, technology and the Global Goals offer a plethora of new opportunities to make this possible. Closing the gender gap alone could add $28 trillion to the global GDP. There's $12 trillion in market opportunities alone within the energy sector, sustainable cities, food and agriculture, and health and well-being. If companies on a large scale take action on the Goals, it will spur the creation of 72 million new jobs in India, 24 million in Latin America and the Caribbean, and 85 million in Africa.

The world is in desperate need of more business leaders with a new set of leadership attributes. You, as new entrepreneurs, are the generation that can make a real difference in the future. And why not begin right here in New York City, the beating heart of sustainable business.

Lise Kingo
Executive Director and CEO of the UN Global Compact

THE
THIRD
WAVE
STEVE CASE
Vote First

Local Community Partner / Tech:NYC

During the past twenty years, New York City's tech sector has grown from a niche market into one of largest tech ecosystems in the world and one of the most important industries in our city and state. Looking forward, it's almost certain this trend will accelerate. This is why, in May 2016, we founded Tech:NYC. We knew our tech and startup communities deserved better representation and stronger connections to each other. Two years later, Tech:NYC represents more than 650 New York tech companies, and our membership continues to expand every month.

NYC's tech sector now represents more than 326,000 jobs, with our startup ecosystem as a whole valued at more than $71 billion. In 2017 alone, the NYC startup ecosystem attracted more than $11.5 billion in funding, up from $2.6 billion in 2012. In the past few years, we've seen many notable milestones, such as the acquisitions of Flatiron Health, AppNexus, Moat, Trello, Meetup and General Assembly, while companies including MongoDB and Yext went public. This is just the beginning.

New York City is one of the most important cities in the world. Our city is a leader in media, finance, real estate, fashion and – of course – innovation. Our world is in the midst of a digital transformation, and, like in all great transformations, the regions, cities and companies that stay ahead of the trends become beacons of growth and progress. New York City is well positioned to continue its leadership by relying on its many assets, including a strong university system, robust capital structure, a diverse and growing talent base, and connections with leaders from other important technology hubs.

Tech:NYC is thrilled to take part in this book, a one-of-a-kind resource that allows anyone – entrepreneurs, investors, workers, explorers – to learn what New York has to offer. We welcome people from all over the world to start their next company here, in one of the greatest cities the world.

Fred Wilson and Tim Armstrong, Co-Chairs
Julie Samuels, Executive Director
Tech:NYC

contents
STARTUP
GUIDE
NEW YORK

startups

programs

spaces

experts

founders

schools

investors

Local Ecosystem

[Key Statistics]

- New York City's startup ecosystem includes more than 7,000 startups.
- The city's industries are highly diverse, with fashion, finance, healthcare, media, real estate and more all playing vital roles in the business and startup communities.
- The NYC tech sector represented 326,000 jobs at the end of 2016.
- NYC's startup ecosystem is valued at $71 billion and is the third most valuable ecosystem in the world.
- 10% of the United States' developers are located in the New York City metro area.
- NYC has more than 100 incubators and accelerators where startups can grow.
- There are more than 200 coworking spaces in NYC, giving new startups room to scale up and thrive.
- New York City has more than 200,000 businesses with 20 or fewer workers each, employing more than 600,000 people total.
- The city has more than 120 universities, with nearly all offering courses for entrepreneurs and technologists.

[Diversity]

- NYC ranks first overall among 50 global cities for its ability to attract and support women entrepreneurs.
- 47% of NYC's technology workers are foreign born, and immigrants make up 46% of the city's workforce as a whole.
- New York City has more than 410,000 women-owned businesses, more than double any other US city.

Sources: Global Startup Ecosystem Report 2018 (Startup Genome); 2016 NYC Tech Ecosystem Study, 2017 update (HR&A); PwC / CB Insights: MoneyTree Report Q4 2017; NYC Developer Hiring Ecosystem Survey 2017 (Stack Overflow); The Technology Sector in New York City, September 2017 (NYS Comptroller); Dell Women Entrepreneur Cities Index, 2017 (Dell); Women-Owned Businesses in the Nation's 25 Largest Cities, 2016 (Center for an Urban Future); Census.gov; Citylab.com.

[City]

New York City, United States

[Statistics:]

Urban population: **8.6 million**
Metropolitan population: **20.3 million**
Area: **302.6 square miles**
GDP: **$1.5 trillion**

[Funding]

- New York City startups attracted 731 venture capital deals in 2017.
- More than 6,100 VC funding rounds have occurred in NYC since 2010.
- Total funding raised by New York startups in 2013, $4.3 billion; 2014, $5.8 billion; 2015, $8.6 billion; 2016, $8.2 billion; and 2017, $11.5 billion

[Notable Exits]

- Handmade and unique goods marketplace Etsy (went public in 2015)
- Online retailer Jet (acquired for $3.3 billion in 2016)
- Digital advertising company Moat (acquired for $850 million in 2017)
- Database-management business MongoDB (went public in 2017)
- Meal-kit-delivery service Plated (acquired for $200 million in 2017)
- Project-management service Trello (acquired for $425 million in 2017)
- Digital knowledge management company Yext (went public in 2017)
- Healthtech company Flatiron Health (acquired for $2 billion in 2018)
- Edtech company General Assembly (acquired for $412 million in 2018)
- Adtech giant AppNexus (acquired for $1.6 billion in 2018)

[Unicorns]

- Coworking company WeWork (valued at $20 billion)
- Enterprise software business Infor (valued at $10 billion)
- Health insurance startup Oscar (valued at $3.2 billion)
- Real estate company Compass (valued at $2.2 billion)
- Medical appointment business Zocdoc (valued at $2 billion)
- Social media management company Sprinklr (valued at $1.8 billion)
- Website building and hosting company Squarespace (valued at $1.7 billion)
- Eyewear startup Warby Parker (valued at $1.7 billion)
- Real-time information and analytics firm Dataminr (valued at $1.6 billion)
- High-tech fitness company Peloton (valued at $1.2 billion)

Intro to the City

The City That Never Sleeps, Gotham, the Big Apple: call it what you will, New York is a city built on dreams. It is at once the embodiment of American ideals as well a universe unto itself. From its iconic skyline and Central Park to its gritty artist lofts, the city has something for everyone – and everyone is here. From its beginnings in the 1600s as a busy Dutch seaport, to the modern, international economic powerhouse that it is today, New York has always been the ultimate destination for those hungry to turn dreams into reality, a rich melting pot of dynamic peoples and cultures all trying to make it in the city.

With a population of 8.6 million, it is by far the biggest city in the US. It's divided into five boroughs: Manhattan, Brooklyn, Queens, Staten Island and the Bronx. Manhattan has historically been the center of commerce and culture, but this has changed in recent years and businesses and coworking spaces abound in the outer boroughs.

The city has recently seen a dramatic uptick in its economy, and the startup scene is booming. In the 2018 Global Startup Ecosystem Report, New York was dubbed the world's second highest performing startup ecosystem, boasting more than seven thousand startups worth over $71 billion in value. There's a built-in network of support programs to help entrepreneurs get their companies up and running, most notably the New York City Economic Development Corporation (NYCEDC), and the opportunities for startups are endless.

Before You Come

Relocating to New York requires a lot of planning, so prepare well in advance. Getting a work visa will take up to six months, so this is your first priority. Contact your consulate for information on what visa will work best for you. New York is quite expensive, so you'll need at least several thousand dollars saved before you arrive. Also, make sure to purchase proper health insurance in advance, usually through a private insurance company in your home country.

Most newcomers don't commit to long-term accommodation before arriving in the city, as rooms are usually rented within days or weeks of being posted, so leave your apartment search until after you arrive. Instead, base yourself at a short-term sublet, hotel or Airbnb to get a better idea of the city before seeking more permanent residence.

Cost of Living

It's no secret that New York is expensive, but if you're resourceful, you can still live a relatively affordable life here. Rent is, of course, the first thing on the mind of every New Yorker. For a room in an apartment with roommates, expect to pay at least $1,000. One-bedroom apartments start at about $1,900 a month and can go over $5,000. However, there are plenty of ways to save money in the city. Trader Joe's provides affordable groceries, and you'll easily find $3–5 beers during happy hour at your local bar. To save on transport costs, riding a bike is a good alternative to a monthly Metro pass. Dining out is mercifully affordable in Brooklyn and Queens, where the food is also spectacular. If you need some inspiration on how to live on less, take a look at brokelyn.com, which is full of ways to live on the cheap.

ONE WAY
ONE WAY

Disney
PRESENTS
THE LION KING
TICKETS AT THE MINSKOFF THEATRE BOX OFFICE
B'WAY & 45th
ONE WAY
44 St
"EVERYBODY KNEW MATILDA WAS GOOD, THEY JUST DIDN'T KNOW HOW GOOD."
Quad HD
BODY WORLDS

Cultural Differences

New Yorkers are a diverse group, but a spirit of individualism and respect for each other's differences unite them all. They tend to be extroverted, unconventional and business-oriented. They have a 'work hard, play hard' approach to life, typically spending fifty plus hours a week working and then enjoying the many cultural activities around NYC in their free time. It's a common misconception that the locals are tough and unfriendly; in reality, most visitors find them extremely open and willing to help. New Yorkers tend to see themselves as progressives and take pride in their diverse communities. They're passionate foodies, love trying out new restaurants, and like to do everything to the max, including drinking. Take your passport with you if you want to be served alcohol, as venues are strict on the twenty-one-and-over drinking age. Tipping is, of course, a large part of the culture, as service industry employees receive the majority of their salary from tips, which is usually 20 percent of the total bill.

Renting an Apartment

Signing a year lease for an apartment in NYC is difficult, as you'll need to show excellent credit and proof of yearly income. You may also pay a hefty deposit and broker fee. Most people choose to sublet to avoid these hassles. These situations may still require a refundable deposit but are more relaxed and usually don't call for much, if any, paperwork. There are a number of websites where you can find apartment or room listings, such spareroom.com, listingsproject.com, hotpads.com and streeteasy.com.

As far as good neighborhoods to live in, Manhattan or places with an easy commute to Manhattan are always best. Check out Williamsburg, Greenpoint, Bushwick, Fort Greene, Crown Heights, Gowanus, Astoria, Long Island City, and Jersey City. If possible, avoid settling yourself in a long-term location off the L train, as a portion of its line to Manhattan will be temporarily suspended in April 2019 for fifteen months for tunnel repairs.

See **Flats and Rentals** page **249**

I LOVE
NEW YORK

Finding a Coworking Space

Dynamic coworking spaces have exploded in NYC over the last few years, and you can find ones to fit most budgets. Most are in Manhattan and Brooklyn, where the startup scene is thriving. WeWork is the corporate king in NYC, with over fifty locations across the city. There's also an all-female-identifying space called The Wing with locations in Manhattan and Brooklyn. Other notable spaces include Company (formerly known as Grand Central Tech), New Lab, The Assemblage, The Yard, Pencilworks, Civic Hall, Bond Collective, Brooklyn Commons and Fueled Collective. To find a coworking space that best suits you, you can also visit The Luminary blog (blog.getcroissant.com), which offers updated lists of affordable coworking spaces; Digital.nyc, which maintains a database of over one hundred coworking spaces; or check out coworkies.com. If you're on a tight budget, you can always join the hordes of freelancers working at coffee shops all over the city. All you need to do is buy a coffee and maybe a sandwich, and you can enjoy the free wifi all day.

See **Spaces** page **84**

Insurance

Even if you're not from the US, you've probably heard about how expensive healthcare is in this country. Monthly premiums and doctor visits cost much more in the US than in other countries, so plan accordingly. Luckily, many countries have insurance plans specifically designed for those travelling to the US, so check out your local plans before you leave.

If you plan to stay long-term, check out what plans New York State has to offer. All citizens and residents are required to have insurance, whether from their home country or purchased in the US. There is mostly only private insurance available, which can only be purchased through the state. New York residents can sign up for state health insurance at nystateofhealth.ny.gov. If your income is low enough, you may qualify for a government subsidy for your monthly premiums (which start at about $430 a month). Also check out zocdoc.com to find healthcare providers.

See **Insurance Companies** page **250**

Visas and Work Permits

It's essential that you look into your visa options at least six months before coming to the US. There are various options, but many come with long processing times and require that you have a great deal of capital. Luckily, there are fantastic resources to help entrepreneurs obtain the right visa (note that it is not possible to come here on a temporary visa and transition to a work visa). First, be sure to contact your own consulate, which can direct you to free services designed specifically for your country. The New York City Department of Small Business Services (www1.nyc.gov/nycbusiness/article/get-free-legal-advice) and the New York City Bar (www.nycbar.org/get-legal-help/) provide similar services. The New York City Economic Development Corporation (NYCEDC) and the City University of New York (CUNY) can help qualified entrepreneurs gain access to an uncapped H-1B visas through the City's IN2NYC program (in2.nyc).

See **Important Government Offices** page **249**

DO NOT
ENTER
DO NOT
ENTER
8'-11"
CLEARANCE
ONE WAY

Taxes

In New York, you must pay city, state, and federal taxes, but there are also some tax incentives for startups. Go to esd.ny.gov/startup-ny-program for information on going tax-free for ten years if you partner with academic organizations, and also check out the Research and Development Tax Credit, which most startups take advantage of. Federal corporate income taxes for C Corporations are due April 18, and Partnership LLC and S Corporation taxes on March 15. All incorporated businesses must pay a state-based Franchise Tax (due in March) and the Payroll Tax if you employ people (usually 10 percent of each employee's salary, due every time they receive a paycheck). Another tax to be aware of is the Sales Tax, which is remitted quarterly or monthly to the state in which a sale takes place.
For more information and for help getting a tax lawyer, contact your consulate and head to www1.nyc.gov/nycbusiness/ie to get a sense of which incentives you might be eligible for using the City's Incentives Estimator.

See **Accountants** page **248**

Starting a Company

Registering your company in the US depends on a number of variables. Usually, companies started by people without a Green Card are registered as a Limited Liability Company (LLC), which automatically registers you with the Internal Revenue Service (IRS) and gets you a Federal Tax ID Number, also known as an Employer Identification Number. You must also register for a State Tax ID Number and file for Foreign Qualification in any other states your company does business in. Check each state's .gov website for more details. You'll also need a Registered Agent (whether it's you or a professional service) to receive official legal documents on behalf of your company. Contact your consulate and the NYCEDC, who can put you in touch with incubators and accelerators that will help you navigate these first steps. For free legal advice and a comprehensive checklist on how to register your company, visit nyc.gov/nycbusiness/. You can also go to upcounsel.com to find an attorney.

See **Programs** page **58**

Opening a Bank Account

To open a personal bank account, you'll need your Social Security Number (SSN), two forms of ID and proof of residency. If you don't have an SSN yet, Santander Bank lets you open a personal account without one. It's also sometimes possible to open an account through one of the following banks in your home country before arriving in the US: Barclays, HSBC, Citibank, Deutsche Bank, and Credit Suisse. For a corporate bank account, the documentation depends on your corporate structure, but you'll usually need either your SSN or your Federal Employee Identification (FEI) number as well as proof that your company has been registered with the IRS. Be aware of the various fees associated with different types of accounts, and have your NYC bank teller explain them to you before choosing one. Your local consulate can also recommend the best bank and type of account for you.

See **Banks** page **248**

& DIAMOND
NEW YORK NYC
NEW YORK CITY
Do I Look like A People Person?
verizon
BURGER KING
Canal St Station
N Q R W
6 at Canal St & Lafayette
J Z at Canal St & Centre
Enter with or buy MetroCard at all times. Agent across Broadway 6am-10pm or see agent at Canal & Lafayette Sts

Getting Around

New York City has by far the largest and busiest public transit system in the US, where most people get around using subways, buses, and commuter rails. The subway alone serves more than 5 million people each weekday and is open twenty-four hours (unlike transit options in other cities in the US). Most New Yorkers have a love-hate relationship with the subway. Due to trains switching routes or changing from local to express and the potential for long delays, locals typically add twenty minutes onto their estimated travel time. A single ride ticket covers the entire subway system and costs about $3, with discounts available for reusable MetroCards. An unlimited weekly card is $32 or a monthly pass is $121. Annoyingly, many ticket machines will take a few tries before reading your card. If paying with a foreign bank card, choose 'debit' (the 'credit' option will ask for a US-based zip code). For maps and info on the latest delays and service changes, download the My Transit app. Remember that locals refer to the subway simply as "the train" or "the subway." There's no Metro here!

The city is also very walkable with easy navigation thanks to its grid layout. Numbers rise south to north, and east to west. The bike-share system is thriving with Citi Bike, and of course Uber and Lyft will happily cart you around. A new network of ferries also opened in 2017, where passengers can enjoy skyline views on their way to work or the beach (ferry.nyc).

Phone and Internet

In the US, there are four major phone carriers – AT&T, Sprint, T-Mobile, Verizon – which all have excellent service in NYC. Most people opt for plans that include unlimited text, talk and data, as New Yorkers tend to spend an exorbitant amount of time on their phones. There are pay-as-you-go plans, but they may come with certain limitations, and monthly plans are almost always more economical. Unlimited text, talk, and data plans with a new phone generally start at about $70 a month, or without a phone at around $50 a month. To compare plans, check out whistleout.com. There are also numerous no-contract monthly plans (e.g. Mint Mobile, Straight Talk, Red Pocket) that piggyback on the infrastructure of a big provider. Google Fi also has some interesting options and offer international texting plans.

Learning the Language

If English is your second language, this is when your years of watching Hollywood movies finally pay off. Even if your English is less than perfect, New York is an easy place to be understood. Half the population doesn't speak English at home, so rest easy that everyone is okay with your accent! To brush up on your skills, check out kaplaninternational.com for English courses or Be Fluent NYC (at befluentnyc.com) for tailored English tutoring.

Don't forget to pick up some fun New York lingo! The only way to tell someone you're going to Manhattan is to say you're headed to "the city." There's no north or south, just "uptown" and "downtown." A little neighborhood grocery store is referred to as a "deli" or "bodega." A slice of pizza is just "a slice," and when waiting in line for one, be sure to say you are "on line."

See **Language Schools** page **251**

Meeting People

Americans are known for their friendliness, but New Yorkers perhaps not as much so. However, you'll find that people are open and certainly love to network. Check out eventbrite.com for networking events in the city. Digital.nyc has a thorough listing of tech events happening across the five boroughs. Meetup.com and shapr.co are also great ways to expand your social and networking circles. Facebook groups and events are also helpful and generalassemb.ly has a wealth of ways for people in the tech industry to connect. And don't forget to take advantage of going to shows, comedy clubs, art openings and other events, especially those put together by various coworking spaces, incubators and accelerators. Bring your business cards, your most positive 'can-do' American attitude, and you're on your way!

See **Startup Events** page **251**

start

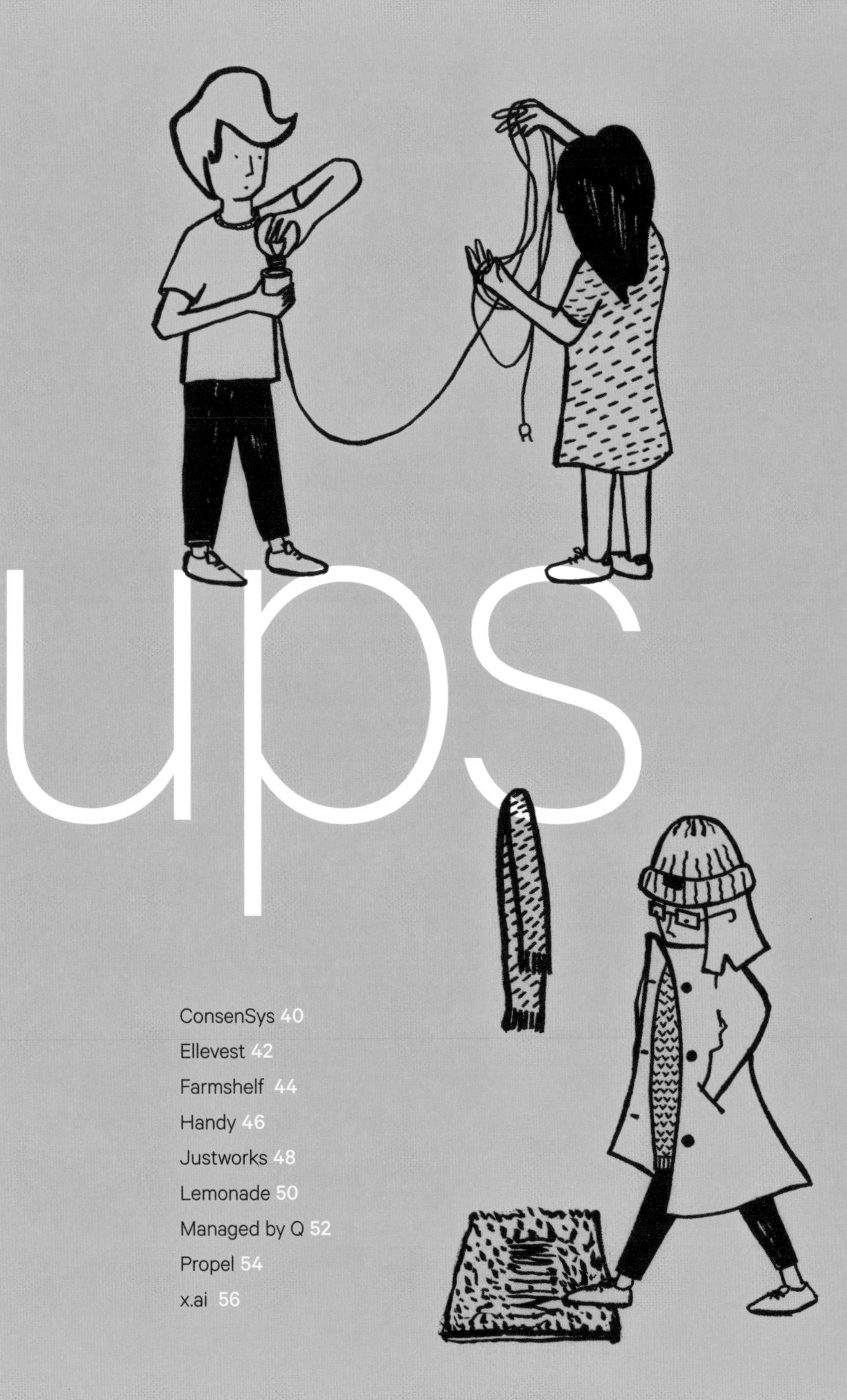

ups

[Name]

ConsenSys

[Elevator Pitch]

"We're a global formation of technologists and entrepreneurs helping to build the Ethereum ecosystem with infrastructure, developer tools, decentralized applications and custom software."

[The Story]

ConsenSys was founded in 2015 by Joseph Lubin, one of the cofounders of the Ethereum blockchain, as a way to help drive Ethereum adoption and grow the network. Lubin believes Ethereum actualizes the early promise of Bitcoin by providing a sophisticated scripting language upon which the blockchain ecosystem can be built. Before launching ConsenSys, Lubin was CEO of Ethereum Switzerland and helped create the nonprofit Ethereum foundation. ConsenSys provides resources, tools and talent to Ethereum entrepreneurs and developers around the world. It also hosts blockchain educational programs, events and gatherings, and provides blockchain consulting services and venture funding. "ConsenSys is the leading global blockchain specialist company," says Amanda Gutterman, chief marketing officer at ConsenSys. "Our goal is to catalyze our transition as a society into a future that is more inclusive, transparent and efficient."

ConsenSys Labs currently houses forty-seven different Ethereum-based projects. Notable projects include MetaMask, a Chrome browser extension that allows you to interact with the blockchain-based web; Truffle, the most popular development framework for Ethereum; and Infura, a scalable blockchain infrastructure that handles 5.6 billion requests each day. "The Ethereum blockchain unlocks business models never before possible," says Amanda. "It increases efficiency in business processes and democratizes access."

[Funding History]

Bootstrap

ConsenSys is privately funded with various internal stakeholders. They have five business domains that operate with different business models and revenue streams that contribute value to the ecosystem, a number of which are cash-flow positive.

[Milestones]

- Reaching five hundred employees in under three years.
- Creating the Blockchain for Social Impact coalition to help address social and environmental challenges.
- Forming the Enterprise Ethereum Alliance to create a roadmap for enterprise features and requirements.
- Becoming the official blockchain advisor to the city of Dubai in March of 2017.
- Becoming the official partner to the EU Blockchain Observatory in February 2018.

[Links]

Web: consensys.net Facebook: consensussystems Twitter: @ConsenSys

ABOUT

[Name]

Ellevest

[Elevator Pitch]

"We're a financial services company that focuses on women. Historically, women report high levels of dissatisfaction with financial services and wealth management – and they've been underserved by those sectors. We aim to be a new kind of financial advisor."

[The Story]

Ellevest was founded on a simple premise: that women have been failed by the financial services industry. According to a 2013 study by AdviceIQ, about 86 percent of financial advisors are male. The Bureau of Labor Statistics data shows that women make less money; Payscale found that their salaries peak earlier, and U.S. Census data show that they live longer than men do. Thus, the National Institute on Retirement Security found that women retire with only two-thirds of the wealth. That's the investing gap: women are simply not investing as much as men. And even when they do, they're more concerned with their personal financial goals than with beating the market.

Ellevest aims to bridge this gap with wealth-management and financial-service tools made by women for women. "This is an industry that does a really good job for men and, as a result, has not done a good job for women," says Charlie Kroll, cofounder and president at Ellevest. "We designed products from the ground up with those differences in mind." Ellevest completed more than two hundred hours of interviews with women, ran more than seven thousand investment simulations, and built a truly diverse team: 70 percent women, 40 percent people of color, and 50 percent of women in tech roles. Their product gives women the tools to manage their financial futures and offers a financial-planning and career-coaching service.

[Funding History]

Bootstrap

Seed

External

Ellevest was bootstrapped during its first six months. After that, it raised its first VC funding through a $10 million seed round alongside Morningstar. After launching a beta product, Costa Ventures led a Series A round of $9 million and Rethink Impact led a $25 million Series B.

[Milestones]

- Raising a $10 million seed round with Morningstar and other private investors.
- Launching our platform from the TechCrunch Disrupt NY 2016 stage.
- Expanding our company to three service levels.
- Rolling out a new impact fund focused on women-owned small businesses.

[Links]

Web: ellevest.com Facebook: ellevesting Twitter: @Ellevest Instagram: ellevest

Want to spend all day managing your portfolio?
Invest in Under 10 Minutes

[Name]

Farmshelf

[Elevator Pitch]

"We build automated, hydroponic growing systems that enable anyone to grow food where they live, work and eat. We see a future where the most highly perishable, highly nutritious crops are grown in a way that's more sustainable and tastes better."

[The Story]

From afar, a Farmshelf system looks like a set of large terrariums, but it's far from decoration; the hydroponic system allows users to grow their own food and offers a vision of the future of sustainable urban farming. Farmshelf can produce fifty different crops at two to three times their normal growth rate while also using significantly less water than traditional farming methods. And it can all be done from the comfort of your home. Farmshelf Founder and CEO Andrew Shearer was inspired to start the company while working at Pinterest. "I started collecting Pinterest boards on how to grow my own food," Andrew says. "With new systems out there, you can empower a whole generation of people to grow their own food and become urban farmers."

How is this possible? A combination of next-level engineering and simply letting nature do its job. "We look at what the plants need on a very basic level: light, nutrients, water, airflow and a certain makeup of the air," Andrew says, "and then we have systems that provides the plant exactly what it needs when it needs it." Farmshelf couldn't come at a more important time. The UN estimates that food production needs to grow by 70 percent by 2050 to feed the world's population. With Farmshelf, Andrew believes that doing this just might be possible.

[Funding History]

Pre-Seed

Seed

Angel

Farmshelf got its start through an accelerator program called Urban-X that aims to solve some of the world's greatest urban challenges and invests up to $100,000 in early-stage startups. It has also received angel funding, including from Chip Bergh, president and CEO of Levi Strauss & Co., and last year it raised its first seed round.

[Milestones]

- **Demoing our first prototype in June 2016 at Urban-X Demo Day.**
- **Installing three Farmshelf prototypes in Grand Central Station in May 2017.**
- **Raising our first round of funding in May 2017.**
- **Increasing the team from four to twelve full-time employees.**

[Links] Web: **farmshelf.com** Facebook: **Farmshelf** Twitter: **@farmshelf** Instagram: **farmshelf**

farmshelf

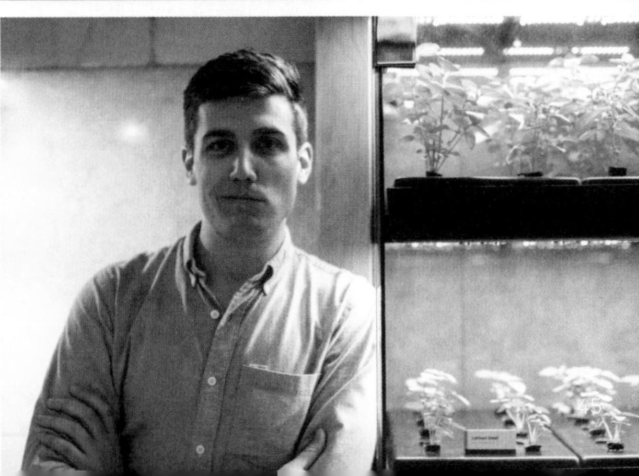

[Name]

Handy

[Elevator Pitch]

"Our goal with Handy is provide every service for every home, ranging from home cleaning and handyperson services to the mounting of your television or helping you set up your smart home."

[The Story]

The idea for Handy began in Budapest, Hungary, where CEO and cofounder Oisin Hanrahan worked as a real-estate developer. While renovating a series of apartments around the city, Oisin found it difficult to find quality handyworkers he could trust to get the job done. Several years later, while attending Harvard Business School, Oisin found that this was also a problem in the US. Together with then-roommate Umang Dua, Oisin set out to create the "Uber for home maintenance." "We started putting up ads around campus offering people the ability to hire our pre-vetted cleaners and handymen and women," explains Oisin, a native of Ireland. "We quickly had dozens and dozens of customers."

In 2012, they raised $50,000 from a venture capital firm to launch the business. After spending the summer in a startup accelerator, the duo moved the business to New York City, where they continued to build their platform and sign up more tradespeople. Today, individuals in the US, UK and Canada can use the Handy app to book everything from home cleaning to furniture assembly. All Handy service professionals are carefully screened, and quality is assured through a customer feedback system. Handy also works with retailers like Walmart and Wayfair to help their customers access convenient television-mounting and furniture-assembly services. To date, Handy has facilitated millions of bookings and served over half a million customers.

[Funding History]

Seed

External

Handy has raised $110 million over seven rounds of funding. It launched with a $50,000 investment from a venture capital firm in 2012, and closed a $12 million Series A in 2013, followed by a $45 million Series B in 2015. Later that year, Handy raised an additional $50 million in a Series C round.

[Milestones]

- **Establishing proof of concept after being met with high customer demand when we launched the business at Harvard.**
- **Seeing similar startups that launched after us close down, which proved that we had the superior business model.**
- **Becoming profitable in the fall of 2017.**
- **Striking partnership deals with brands like Walmart and Wayfair, because it showed that our core business was strong enough and we were ready to expand.**

[Links]

Web: **handy.com** Facebook: **handyhq** Twitter: **@Handy** Instagram: **handy_hq**

handy

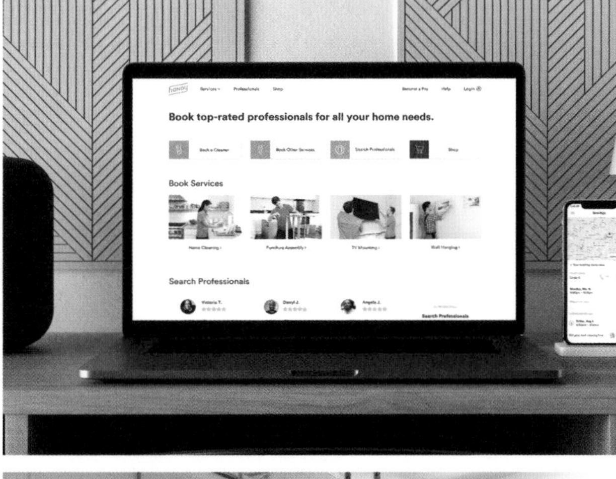
Book top-rated professionals for all your home needs.
Book Services
Search Professionals

[Name]

Justworks

[Elevator Pitch]

"We help entrepreneurs and businesses grow with confidence by giving them access to big-company benefits, automated payroll, HR tools and compliance support – all in one place."

[The Story]

Justworks is building a world in which starting, running and joining a growing businesses is an accessible option for all. It does this by combining the power of a certified professional employer organization (PEO) with exceptional 24/7 customer service and a simple and inviting platform, so teams of all sizes can work fearlessly, pursue their passion and do more of what matters.

For Isaac Oates, founder and CEO of Justworks, this idea was born out of personal experience. At his first startup Adtuitive (a contextually driven ad platform for retailers) and later at Etsy (which acquired Adtuitive), Isaac was struck by "how manual and antiquated" the process of setting up and managing core business infrastructure was. He wasn't alone. "I'd spoken to entrepreneurs in different sectors, and they all came back to this as a huge pain point," Isaac says. "If we could build something for entrepreneurs to hire, pay and take care of their people, it would be a huge improvement – and ultimately let them focus on building great businesses." Founded in 2012, Justworks now offers access to benefits, payroll, HR tools and compliance support for businesses in all fifty US states. "We're really proud of the role that we play," Isaac says. "Not only are we growing, but we also support other companies' growth."

[Funding History]

Seed Angel External

After a $1 million seed round, Justworks has raised four additional rounds of venture capital financing: a $6 million Series A led by Thrive Capital, $13 million Series B led by Bain Capital Ventures, $33 million Series C led by Redpoint Ventures, and $40 million Series D led by First Mark Capital. Other backers include Index Ventures and Spark Capital.

[Milestones]

- **Building and testing a beta product in April 2013.**
- **Launching the full benefits platform in 2015.**
- **Running the first Justworks ad campaign on the NYC subway.**
- **Reaching four hundred employees in 2018.**

[Links] Web: **justworks.com** Facebook: **JustworksHR** Twitter: **@JustworksHR** Instagram: **justworks_hr**

Alerts
Today
Upcoming documents

[Name]

Lemonade

[Elevator Pitch]

"We're a new kind of insurance company built from the ground up using behavioral economics and artificial intelligence, and driven by social good."

[The Story]

When entrepreneurs Daniel Schreiber and Shai Wininger looked at the insurance landscape in the US, they saw a mess – and within that mess, an opportunity. Insurance affected hundreds of millions people and moved trillions of dollars each year, but the industry was dominated by companies founded during the age of the horse-drawn carriage (State Farm, Allstate, Progressive), and these companies were consistently maligned. "Combine those three – huge, unchanged and unloved – and you've got the conditions for a disruptive startup to emerge," says Daniel, cofounder and CEO of Lemonade.

Founded in 2015, Lemonade was designed with the aim of making insurance more human – by using chatbots and behavioral economics, naturally. Unlike other insurance companies, which make money by denying or delaying claims, Lemonade takes a flat fee out of your monthly payment: no more, no less. This, along with AI technology, allows it to settle claims more quickly, usually within a day or even faster. Lemonade is also a certified B corporation that donates a portion of its profits to charity. Unclaimed money doesn't go to Lemonade but rather to a charity organization of the customer's choosing. "Give back and social mission is really very core to what we do," Daniel says. "Once you've nullified the financial incentive, once I've got no incentive to deny your claim, then technology can do some pretty amazing stuff."

[Funding History]

Seed

External

Lemonade raised its first round of seed funding with Sequoia Capital and Aleph in 2015. It has since raised Series A ($13 million), B ($34 million), and C ($120 million) rounds, alongside companies including XL, General Catalyst, Softbank, Google Ventures, and others.

[Milestones]

- **Raising $13 million in seed funding with Sequoia in December 2015.**
- **Launching product and becoming a certified insurance carrier in the state of New York.**
- **Becoming available to almost 60 percent of the US population within a span of twenty months.**
- **Seeing 1,000 percent year-on-year growth in first half of 2018.**

[Links] Web: **lemonade.com** Facebook: **Lemonade** Twitter: **@Lemonade_Inc** Instagram: **lemonade_inc**

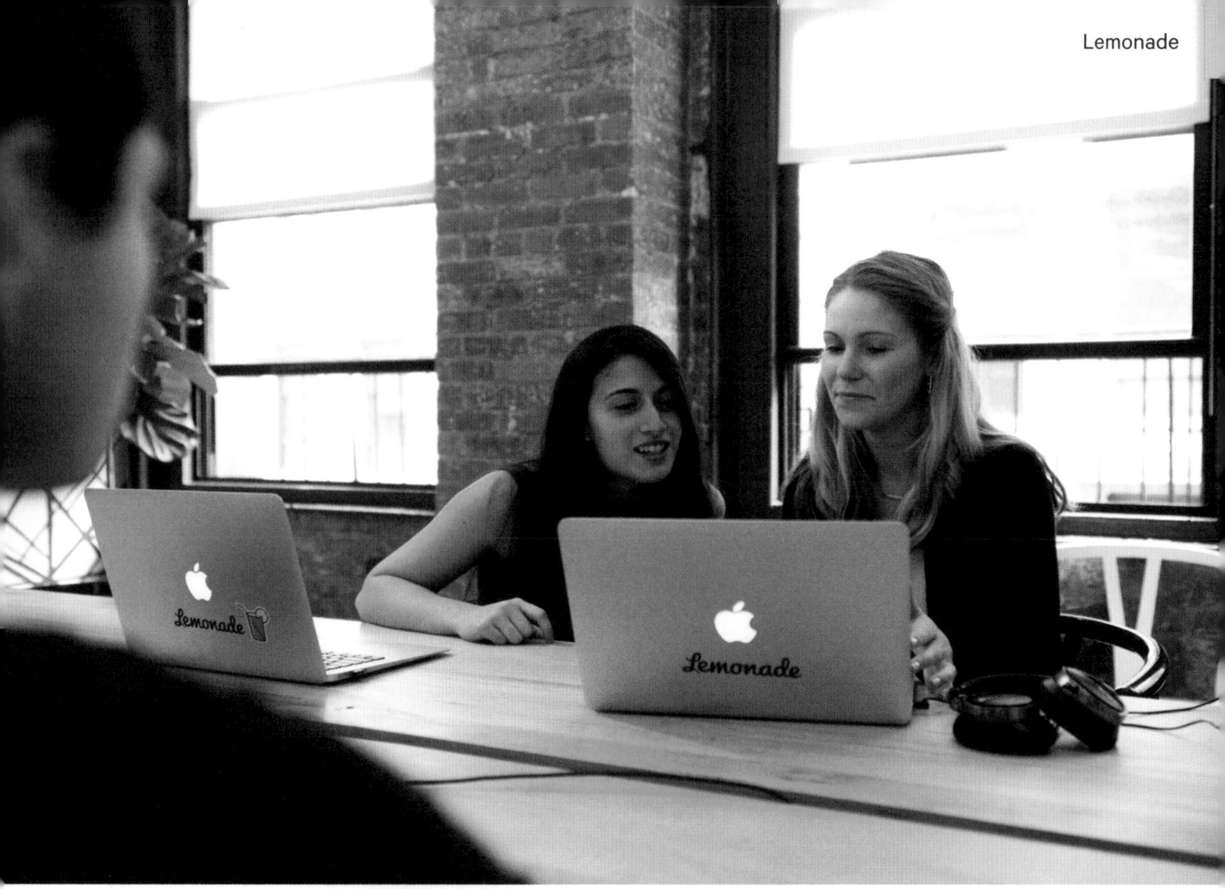

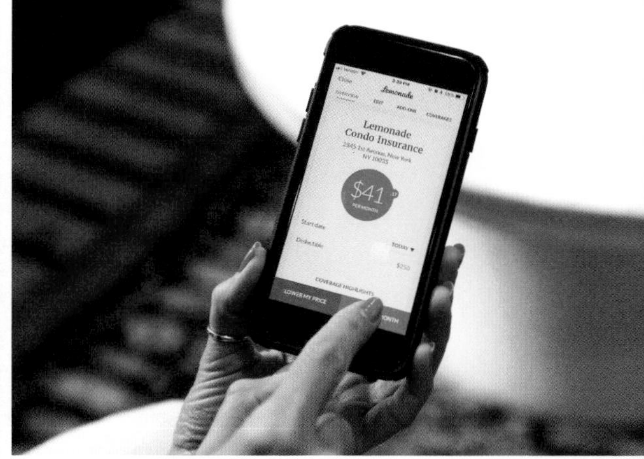
Lemonade
Condo Insurance
$41

[Name]

Managed by Q

[Elevator Pitch]

"We help the world's leading companies run their workplaces through our integrated platform where you can source, book, manage, and pay for the best local office service providers."

[The Story]

When Managed by Q launched, Dan Teran had little experience in facilities management, but his work at a venture development firm made him acutely aware that businesses weren't being run efficiently. "I had a front-row seat to the challenges of starting a company and office," Dan says. "So we started kicking around the idea of an operating system for a physical space that could run with the reliability of software." Dan and cofounder Saman Rahmanian rented an office space in NYC's Chinatown and built Managed by Q, named in reference to "the talkative genius who creates all the tools that allow James Bond to do his work."

Managed by Q offers cleaning, maintenance and supply services, IT, security, administrative staffing, and project management to offices. The key to its success is the technology platform, which connects businesses to hundreds of vetted service providers and allows clients to organize their service-provider bookings, communication, management, and payments all in one place. "We think of it as Amazon Web Services for the office space," Dan says. "A complex coordination of people, processes and technology that creates outcomes in the real world." Today, Managed by Q has operations throughout the US and works with thousands of companies from Fortune 500 businesses to startups. It offers benefits and equity to all employees, regardless of their role, and has been recognized for its commitment to economic empowerment.

[Funding History]

Seed

Angel

External

Managed by Q has raised $72.4 million over five funding rounds, starting with $775,000 from an angel round in 2014 and an additional $1.7 million seed round the same year, then a $10 million Series A in 2015, a $25 million Series B in 2016, and another $30 million Series C later that year.

[Milestones]

- Launching Managed by Q in April 2014.
- Announcing the "Operator Stock Option Program," which offers equity to employees at all levels of the company.
- Managed by Q's service company, Q Services, becoming profitable in October of 2017.
- Acquiring Hivy, an internal office communications startup.
- Acquiring NVS, a real estate services firm specializing in pre-lease planning, project management, and facilities management.

[Links] Web: managedbyq.com Facebook: ManagedbyQ Twitter: @ManagedbyQ Instagram: managedbyq

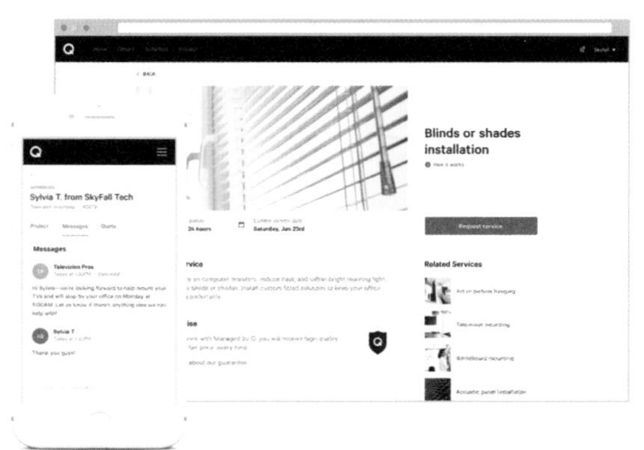
Blinds or shades installation
Sylvia T. from SkyFall Tech
Messages
Related Services

[Name]

Propel

[Elevator Pitch]

"We build financial software for people on food stamps. Our goal is to make America's safety net more user-friendly so that somebody who runs into financial trouble has a modern and respectful way to get back on their feet."

[The Story]

More than forty million Americans, or just under 15 percent of the US population, are on food stamps, but simply checking one's food stamp balance can be surprisingly difficult. Food stamp recipients buy their groceries with an Electronic Benefits Transfer (EBT) card, which is like a credit card except for one shortcoming: you can't check your balance online. This leaves two options: save grocery store receipts or call a hotline. Propel, founded in 2014, offers a third way. Propel created a phone app called Fresh EBT that lets people on food stamps check their balance, manage their benefits, download coupons, apply for work, access community resources, and ultimately keep more money in their pockets – all through their smartphones.

"It's hard to know how to set a budget, or how much food you can buy, when you don't know how much you have left on your card," says Jimmy Chen, founder and CEO of Propel. Fresh EBT aims to address the rising gap between the developers and end-users of software and now has more than one million monthly active users. Ultimately, the app is showing that technology can not only benefit the well-off but also play a role in supporting those living in poverty, too.

[Funding History]

Bootstrap

Seed

External

Propel began in the lab, specifically, the Blue Ridge Labs @ Robin Hood Foundation. Propel was bootstrapped through Blue Ridge, a program that develops startups aimed at addressing economic inequality, but it has since expanded its funding to include institutional funding from venture capitalists, external funding from nonprofits and revenue generated as a social business.

[Milestones]

- Reaching 1 million active users in January 2018.
- Eclipsing $4 million in money saved by users.
- Raising $4 million in seed funding from VC investors in April 2017.
- Supporting 12,000 job applications by app users to food service and other job providers.

[Links]

Web: joinpropel.com Facebook: freshEBT Twitter: @freshebt Instagram: freshebt

My Spending
SEPTEMBER 2016

[Name]

x.ai

[Elevator Pitch]

"We schedule meetings for you using an AI agent."

[The Story]

After selling his last business in 2013, x.ai founder and CEO Dennis Mortensen looked back through his calendar from the previous year, and what he saw amazed him: of the 1,019 meetings he had scheduled, 672 of them had to be rescheduled. "If you win the corporate lottery and get a human assistant to manage your calendar, you're just moving the chore of scheduling meetings from one person to another," Dennis said. "I wanted to see if we could remove the pain altogether and make meeting-scheduling a machine task at machine costs."

Dennis put together a team in 2014 and spent the next two and a half years acquiring funding, performing research and developing the product. In early 2017, they moved out of beta and introduced to the world the commercial versions of Amy and Andrew Ingram: autonomous AI assistants who schedule meetings for you. "Whenever you get an email asking you to get together," explains Dennis, "you can simply respond to that email as usual and cc in amy@x.ai or andrew@x.ai, telling them to help put something on your calendar at a time that works for you and the guest, and then they'll take care of the rest." To date, x.ai has scheduled hundreds of thousands of meetings across the United States.

[Funding History]

Bootstrap

Seed

External

x.ai has raised $44.3 million over four rounds of funding. After initially bootstrapping, the company raised $2.1 million in seed funding in May of 2015, followed by a $9.2 million Series A later that year. In 2016 and 2017, x.ai raised another $33 million in a Series B round.

[Milestones]

- **Assembling the team from my previous business Visual Revenue to help me launch this product.**
- **Launching a commercial version of our product in October 2016.**
- **Expanding with a large remote data labeling team in Manila in January 2017.**
- **Adding features to Amy and Andrew to allow for the scheduling of team meetings (i.e., meetings between more than two individuals).**

[Links] Web: **x.ai** Facebook: **xdotai** Twitter: **@xdotai** Instagram: **xdotai**

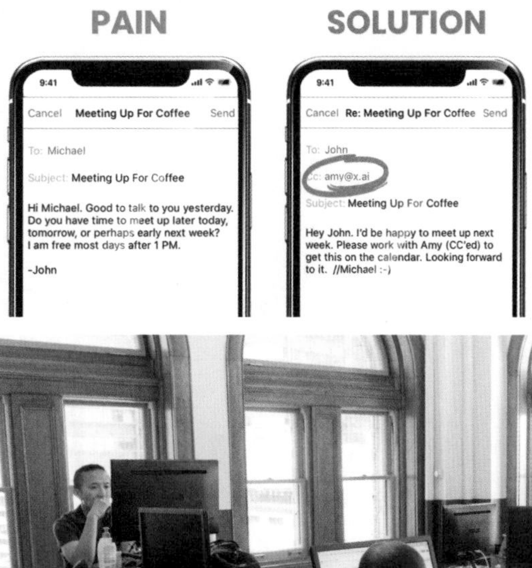

PAIN

9:41

Cancel Meeting Up For Coffee Send

To: Michael

Subject: Meeting Up For Coffee

Hi Michael. Good to talk to you yesterday. Do you have time to meet up later today, tomorrow, or perhaps early next week? I am free most days after 1 PM.

-John

SOLUTION

9:41

Cancel Re: Meeting Up For Coffee Send

To: John

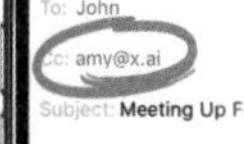

Subject: Meeting Up For Coffee

Hey John. I'd be happy to meet up next week. Please work with Amy (CC'ed) to get this on the calendar. Looking forward to it. //Michael :-)

prog

rams

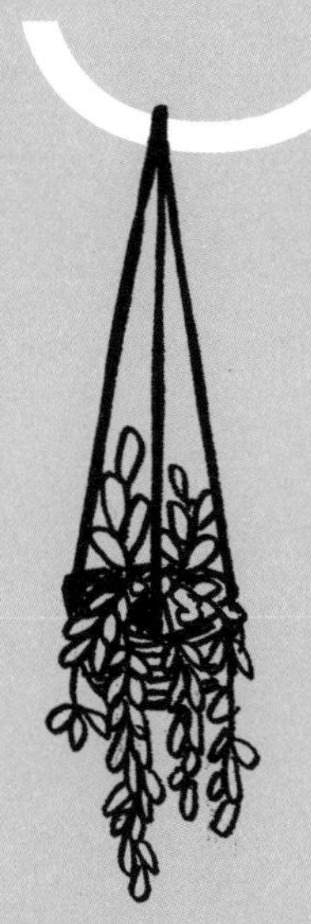

- **Have a bias toward action.**
  We're looking for people who don't just do the research or talk about change but go out and actually do things to make it happen.

- **Be in New York.**
  We're looking for companies and founders that are either already operating out of New York City or expect to be in New York in the next one to two years.

- **Have an established skill set.**
  We're looking for somebody who has a robust portfolio. For example, if you're a designer, we'd like you to have at least a few years of experience under your belt.

- **Be adaptable and receptive to feedback.**
  Starting a company is an exercise in constantly being told that you're wrong. View that as opportunity for learning and growth.

- **Focus on the community.**
  We want to see that people are building products or services that will benefit low-income communities.

[Name]

Blue Ridge Labs @ Robin Hood

[Elevator Pitch]

"We're an initiative of the Robin Hood Foundation that asks how technology can contribute to measurably and sustainably lifting New York City families out of poverty."

[Sector]

Social Venture

[Description]

Blue Ridge Labs @ Robin Hood was founded on the simple premise that the people closest to New York City's greatest problems – such as rising rents and gentrification, the school-to-prison pipeline, and other social justice issues – are also the people closest to the solutions. "We looked out at the world, and we saw tech being used in lots of ways to improve the lives of folks at the high end of the income spectrum," says Hannah Calhoon, managing director at Blue Ridge Labs @ Robin Hood. "We didn't see platforms or services that were helping the people who absolutely needed it the most."

Blue Ridge Labs aims to democratize the benefits of technology by working for and with the community it seeks to serve. It does this through two flagship programs – the Blue Ridge Labs @ Robin Hood Fellowship and the Catalyst program – and through an in-house Design Insight Group. The first offering, the Fellowship program, brings together technologists, designers, entrepreneurs and topic experts to spend four months exploring and launching new products. Out of this program have emerged both for-profit and nonprofit ventures that allow low-income New Yorkers to do everything from fighting evictions to checking their food-stamps balance. Blue Ridge's other program, called Catalyst, is a six-month incubator that provides funding, space, mentoring, and networking opportunities to early-stage startups that are aiming to create social change.

The organization places a premium on listening to the community, which is why it also runs the Design Insight Group, a community of more than nine hundred low-income community members who participate in paid research opportunities – everything from interviews and focus groups to product testing and surveys. "We believe that the best tech solutions come from getting technologists out into the community to have conversations and to work with people on the front lines who have spent decades of their lives doing this," Hannah says.

[Apply to]

labs.robinhood.org

[Links]

Web: **labs.robinhood.org** Twitter: **@BlueRidgeLabs**

- **Assemble a great team.**
  We base around 80 percent of our selection decision on the team. If we find a great team but the idea is questionable, we don't hesitate to invest in them, because we know that the team will make things work.

- **Pick a growth market.**
  We base around 15 percent of our decision on the market size. If a company can be successful in New York City, and if New York City has the right industries for a startup, then we invest in that company.

- **Have a great idea.**
  We base the remaining 5 percent on the idea. A great team can always change its idea.

- **Get to know the right people.**
  We get a lot of referrals through our network of graduate companies. They know how we work, how hands on we are, and how much value we bring, so they often come to us with referrals.

[Name]

Entrepreneurs Roundtable Accelerator

[Elevator Pitch]

"We're an early-stage venture capital fund and accelerator in New York City. We take a holistic approach to helping the companies that we invest in, providing mentoring in anything that the startup requires."

[Sector]

Multiple

[Description]

Entrepreneurs Roundtable Accelerator (ERA) is New York's leading tech accelerator with more than 150 alumni, 400 mentors, 50 corporate partners, $300 million raised and $2 billion in market cap. ERA connects early-stage startups with mentors, invests in their innovations, and provides them with up to $1 million worth of free resources, such as web-hosting, legal work and accounting services.

But despite its current largesse, ERA came out of humble roots. In fact, when it first started out more than a decade ago, it just was a small nonprofit trying to bring together a dispersed startup community.

"These days, New York is a great place for startups," says cofounder and managing partner of ERA Murat Aktihanoglu, "but in 2007, the network was not formed yet. The community was very dispersed, and people didn't know each other. Investors couldn't find startups, and startups couldn't find investors." Realizing this need, Aktihanoglu and ERA cofounder John Axelrod began to organize free monthly get-togethers to bring startups and investors into the same room as one another. Three years later, they launched ERA as the city's first-ever accelerator. ERA has since graduated 165 startups and now runs two four-month courses each year. Admission to the program is highly selective. According to Aktihanoglu, out of more than one thousand applicants for each course, just twelve to fourteen are admitted.

Making it into this select group comes with elite benefits. Right off the bat, ERA invests an initial $100,000 in companies, with the possibility of further investments down the road. "Once we're invested in a company, we do everything for them," Aktihanoglu says. Startups receive mentoring services as well as partner and sponsor benefits from the likes of Microsoft, Apple, Google, and Stripe. Then, at the end of their four months, they have the opportunity to present their innovations to more than one thousand potential investors at Demo Days, the largest event of its kind on the East Coast.

[Apply to]

eranyc.com/apply

[Links]

Web: **eranyc.com** Facebook: **groups/eroundtable** Twitter: **@ERoundtable**

- **Take the test.**
  We have a personality test that benchmarks your core personality against that of a successful entrepreneur. Doing a really good job on the test is the best way to get into the program. We're looking for things like high openness, high fluid intelligence, moderate agreeableness, and so on.

- **Be scrappy.**
  Our admissions process is designed to identify founders that have the openness, determination and problem-solving skills to adapt and build a great company.

- **Don't be a stranger.**
  We host free events, and we're out in the community. Make yourself known and just come say hi.

[Name]

Founder Institute

[Elevator Pitch]

"We're the world's largest launch-stage accelerator. We help companies pre-seed – from as early as when they have an idea – through a fourteen-week mentorship program alongside experienced founders and CEOs."

[Sector]

Multiple

[Description]

To be the best, you must surround yourself with the best, and for early-stage startups, Founder Institute is the right place to do this. Founded in 2009 in Silicon Valley, Founder Institute runs early-stage, pre-seed accelerator programs in more than two hundred cities around the world. The idea is simple: to find individuals with an entrepreneurial spirit and drive and connect them to mentors with years of experience in the field. Over the course of fourteen weeks, founders connect with CEOs, entrepreneurs and industry experts at weekly presentations and working groups and, of course, over drinks. Each week covers a different element of starting a company, from revenue modeling to bootstrapping and fundraising, and takes founders all the way from idea to business to launch. "By the end of the fourteen weeks, you have a solid foundation to build, launch and grow your company," says Kevin Siskar, managing director of the Founder Institute New York.

The program, founded by entrepreneur and New York native Adeo Ressi alongside colleague Jonathan Greechan, emerged as a response to the lack of mentorship opportunities for early-stage founders. It has helped launch more than three thousand companies, who have raised around $700 million in startup funds and together are worth nearly $20 billion. About 175 portfolio companies have emerged from the New York chapter since 2009, ranging from SimpleReach, a cloud platform for content marketing optimization, to Easy Aerial, a smart security system run by drones. Founder Institute also hosts a monthly New York meetup open to the public and runs a Bonus Pool, allowing graduates to invest in not just their own company but their peers' as well. For budding entrepreneurs, these services provide the necessary push to build the next great company. "You don't need to build some super sexy platform right away," Kevin says. "You can just start the business. The best founders just get going, and they're scrappy as hell."

[Apply to] **fi.co/join/admissions**

[Links] Website: **fi.co** Facebook: **FounderInstitute** Twitter: **@founding** Instagram: **founding**

- **Have prior (self-taught) experience.**
  We test for both passion and signs they've done some of the early work themselves.

- **Bring your past skills with you.**
  We love people who have been good at something else and are at the top of their field.

- **Be a learner and a teacher.**
  The best way to learn something is to teach it. You won't learn the fundamentals unless you get your hands dirty and build something – and then explain how you did it to your classmates.

- **Clear your schedule.**
  Fullstack is a very intense experience that requires all your focus – and then some.

- **Prepare for admissions with Fullstack's Bootcamp Prep.**
  The best way to prepare for the admissions assessment is a Bootcamp Prep course. For a fraction of the cost of the full-time program, you can build the foundations you need over week- and month-long courses (in person and online).

[Name]

Fullstack Academy

[Elevator Pitch]

"We're a coding boot camp, and our pitch is 'three months to a new job in tech.' Our goal is to find people who are passionate about transforming their careers and get them working in the next wave of industry-changing tech."

[Sector]

IT

[Description]

Coding is not for the faint of heart, but that doesn't mean it can't be for everyone. At Fullstack, neophyte coders across different industries and from all walks of life can jump into the world of programming and see if they sink or swim. A coding "bootcamp" with locations in New York, Chicago, and online, Fullstack aims to create the next generation of great coders. Founded by David Yang and Nimit Maru, who together have nearly thirty-five years of coding experience, Fullstack offers an intensive seventeen-week training program called the Software Engineering Immersive, an all-women's boot camp called the Grace Hopper Program, a part-time Flex option, and a college-level summer program. "Since our founding, we've graduated fifteen hundred students," says Yang, cofounder and CEO of Fullstack. "An impressive number of companies in the New York, Chicago and San Francisco ecosystems have a Fullstack student – or even a cadre of them – embedded there."

David and Nimit, who first met as undergraduates, founded the program to address what they saw as a talent gap across the United States. The program doesn't draw just from STEM fields but attracts candidates across multiple industries, from finance and law to journalism and design. To best train this wide range of students, Fullstack teaches JavaScript, which allows for relatively new coders to jump into the profession without having to learn the complex syntax of other systems. "America needs to build a talent pool in really short order," Yang says. "The tech world needs people who can bring external ideas to the table."

Alongside the technical skills it teaches, Fullstack also focuses on student development and career services, ultimately equipping students with a ready-made network once they graduate. "If you're looking to make a move into a city and an industry," says David, "a bootcamp is a great way to learn a skill that's both in high demand and optimized for that particular community."

[Apply to]

fullstackacademy.com/apply

[Links]

Web: **fullstackacademy.com** Facebook: **FullstackAcademy** Twitter: **@fullstack**

- **Do your research.**
  If you want to prep for the program, you should already have done some research on your own, and you should have a sense of what day-to-day life is like for a professional in the field you're studying.

- **Fully commit to the program.**
  We look for students who are self-driven, because the program is immersive. We're teaching you highly complex skills in a very short time period.

- **Be career-ready.**
  This is a program for career-focused people. For part-time programs, we're looking for professionals who already have some aptitude or skills that they're looking to improve.

- **Develop a baseline of skills.**
  This isn't a program for neophytes. If you're applying to the coding course, for example, you should at least have tried your hand at code before starting.

[Name]

General Assembly

[Elevator Pitch]

"We're advancing the future of work by equipping individuals and organizations with the most in-demand twenty-first-century skills. Offering training and assessments in web development, data science, digital marketing, and more, we're building transparent career pathways for people, and sustainable, diverse talent pipelines for employers."

[Sector]

IT

[Description]

Perhaps more so than any of New York's established educational programs, General Assembly is uniquely suited to teach graduates the skills to run a startup or to lead teams. That's because the program itself is a product of the startup ecosystem. General Assembly, which occupies three stories in the heart of Manhattan's Flatiron district, started as a coworking space in 2011. Seven years later, it has become a truly global school with twenty campuses and over forty thousand graduates around the world. The school offers three full-time intensive courses (ten to twelve weeks each) in web development, data science, and user experience design, as well as part-time courses in everything from javascript development to front-end web development, digital marketing and data analytics. "New York is in our blood as a company," says Mickey Slevin, New York regional director at General Assembly. "Being founded in New York, our growth has been a success story for the city's tech scene, but even better is that our services help other startups fill their talent gaps as they scale and develop their people."

With minimalist classrooms that feature floor-to-ceiling whiteboard walls, expansive shared student workspaces, and a range of events open to the public, General Assembly cultivates an ethos of collaboration within and beyond the walls of the school. About 20 percent of full-time students are supported by scholarships or through social impact programs developed in partnership with the city, state and local nonprofits, according to Slevin.

Though the majority of its students fall into the twenty-five to thirty-five age range, the program is age-agnostic, and students older than sixty have completed full-time programs there. "The future of work is that people will constantly be upskilling and reskilling," Slevin says. "We provide students the courses to keep up and employees the resources to stay current as the landscape shifts."

[Apply to]

generalassemb.ly

[Links]

Web: **generalassemb.ly** Facebook: **generalassembly** Twitter: **@GA** Instagram: **generalassembly**

- **Have a developed idea and business model.**
  Because we work with later-stage founders and take no equity, our companies tend to have more evolved concepts.

- **Room to grow.**
  Our approach to how we program the accelerator is community-driven as opposed to user-driven. We ask our companies where they're struggling and how they can be helped, and execute programming to provide them the answers they need.

- **Be a good company and be a decent company.**
  We're not just looking for highly capable people but also decent people committed to being a part of an organization that has outstanding values, including in recruiting and hiring talent from diverse backgrounds.

- **Diversity wins.**
  We want everybody – especially women and people of color – to know that they're welcome here.

[Name]

Grand Central Tech

[Elevator Pitch]

"Operating out of a fifteen-thousand-square-foot space right next to Grand Central Station, we're a tech accelerator for later-stage founders that doesn't take equity from founders."

[Sector] **Multiple**

[Description]

Sometimes the best way to get ahead is to put yourself right where the action is, and in New York City, there may be no place with more action than the illustrious Grand Central Station. Adjoining this train station is Grand Central Tech, a startup accelerator that helps later-stage startups build, refine and market technology products across multiple industries. Perhaps the most unique element of Grand Central Tech is the fact that the accelerator takes no equity, meaning the profits a company earns stay right with them. "A program that requires seven to ten percent of a company's equity? That's kind of becoming a relic," says Matt Harrigan, CEO and cofounder of Grand Central Tech. "What we're seeing is more and more demand for this alternative model."

Getting into the program is tough, but once a company is in, Grand Central Tech offers unparalleled benefits: one year of free rent in the heart of Midtown; community-led programming to help the company focus in on getting to the next level; and networking opportunities with some of New York's biggest VC firms and corporate partners. "The most critical value added is time," Matt says. "But offering a year's worth of real estate in New York City is no small benefit, and nor are curated experiences or a routine and advantageous introduction to the venture ecosystem in New York."

Grand Central Tech is located in within Company, a coworking space of 1.1 million square feet at 335 Madison Ave. It features thirty-foot-tall ceilings, a stunning view into Grand Central Station, nine conference rooms, three call rooms, kitchens, a lounge area, a gym, a bar, a library, and a theater, to name just a few amenities. "It's one large innovation ecosystem," Matt says. "There might be cooler neighborhoods, but there are no more convenient locations. Our companies understand that being located here helps them secure talent and interact with the corporate world better than anywhere else."

[Apply to] **company.co; application available in September**

[Links] Web: **company.co** Facebook: **GrandCentralTech** Twitter: **@Company** Instagram: **company**

- **Fit into the desired categories.**
  Generally, we're looking at three different categories: very-early-stage startups announcing a new product to the world; larger companies that want to showcase cool, new technology that they're launching for developers; and returning demoers.

- **Have the "wow" factor.**
  Is what you're presenting something that's groundbreaking, unique and different from other technologies?

- **Make an impact.**
  Does your product use technology in a unique way? If the technology itself is not amazing, is it being used in an interesting way? How does it impact its end users?

- **Meet extraneous requirements.**
  Alongside the technology itself, we also look at factors such as potential investment, interest, hiring and user adoption.

[Name]
NY Tech Alliance

[Elevator Pitch] *"We're a 501(c)6 nonprofit organization with the mission to represent, inspire, support and help lead the New York technology community and enhance the overall tech ecosystem to create a better future for all."*

[Sector] **Hardware, software, enterprise**

[Description] In a city where everyone is constantly iterating and inventing, having a place to showcase these inventions is critical. The NY Tech Alliance provides this space through the NY Tech Meetup (NYTM), a monthly demonstration of what's new and cutting edge in the New York tech community. Started in 2004 as an informal gathering of four people in the back office of Meetup, NYTM now brings together thousands of interested technologists each year in locations across the city. Each month, startups and founders can apply to showcase their work in front of 300–350 people. The companies range from startups to established companies, with innovations spanning software to hardware, and media to robotics. "What differentiates us is we focus on the technology itself, how it's being used, and what the implications are," says Andy Saldaña, director of operations at the NY Tech Alliance. "It's more of a 'show and tell' of new technology."

The monthly meetups are just part of what the Alliance does. NYTM merged with the New York Technology Council in 2016 to form the New York Tech Alliance. It now has more than sixty thousand individual and institutional members and hosts events across the city, many of which focus on emerging themes in the tech ecosystem, such as blockchain, AI and civic tech. The Alliance, led by President Erik Grimmelmann and chaired by Andrew Rasiej, ultimately strives to be a go-to resource for people interested in dipping their toes into the tech world in New York. It provides everything from legal advice to programs focused on increasing female, minority, and LGBTQ representation in the tech world. "Even though we represent a huge and broad tech ecosystem," Andy says, "a lot of what we do and what the people who work here do is make sure that any entrepreneur who is in New York and looking to navigate the system has the resources available to connect to the tech ecosystem."

[Apply to] **nytech.org/present**

[Links] Web: **nytech.org** Facebook: **nytechmeetup** Twitter: **@NYTechAlliance**

- **Fit the criteria.**
  The team should have some sort of core connection in the university system. The program is open to students, either in universities or recently graduated, as well as faculty and staff.

- **Demonstrate a commitment to entrepreneurship.**
  One of the things we look for is some sort of significant evidence that you're committed to the idea of being an entrepreneur. A lot of the time it's about where you're at in life and what you understand of the challenge of starting a company, and it's often about the team.

- **Bring in technology talent.**
  The teams we look for have to have some sort of technology talent – some sort of ability to execute on the thing you've said you want to do.

- **Make an impact.**
  It's important to think critically about the implications of the things you build.

[Name]

NYC Media Lab

[Elevator Pitch]

"We're a New York City consortium of universities and industries that's devoted to encouraging emerging media technology, innovation and entrepreneurship."

[Sector]

Media, AI, data science

[Description]

NYC Media Lab companies are revolutionizing the media and tech landscapes, from a company that automates the extraction of information out of videos through AI and machine learning (Vidrovr) to a media platform for meditation (Aduri) to a brain–computer interface for self-driving cars (Braiq). And the crazy part is that most of the companies are founded by recent college graduates. NYC Media Lab generally approaches and develops very-early-stage startups, which means it meets budding entrepreneurs where they are. "A lot of times, we're dealing with relatively inexperienced entrepreneurs," says Justin Hendrix, executive director of NYC Media Lab, "and often part of it is educating them about what being an entrepreneur is, and how that differs from pursuing an academic path or working in a large corporation or government sectors."

NYC Media Lab, created out of a partnership between New York City's top universities, the New York City Economic Development Corporation, and the Mayor's Office of Media and Entertainment, is now in its eighth year and just graduated its third cohort of teams from the Combine, its accelerator program. "The thing all our teams have in common is they're focused on novel applications of data science in media, as well as augmented and virtual reality," says Justin. "The thing we're doing that's a little different is that we've built this community of corporate executives, investors and entrepreneurs that can engage with the startups we bring through the cohort to create a nurturing environment for them."

Along with its accelerator, NYC Media Lab hosts a number of events and demo days, such as Machine + Media, and Exploring Future Reality; and it partners with industry players, including Viacom, *The Associated Press*, and Bloomberg. "Media is such a systemically important industry here in New York," Justin says. "It employs so many tens of thousands of people that it's vital for the economy for us to continue to see new firms succeed and create value."

[Apply to]

thecombine.nyc

[Links]

Web: **nycmedialab.org** Medium: **@nycmedialab** Twitter: **@nycmedialab** YouTube: **nycmedialab**

- **Browse around.**
  We're very aware that we're a government-transparency initiative, so we want to make sure that folks can access this information without having to log in, create a profile, or tell us who they are or what they're looking to do with the data.

- **Support economic development.**
  NYC Open Data was born with an economic development rationale: that by putting city data out and to the public, it would help spur job growth and provide startups with an asset that they could take to develop new applications.

- **Be a problem-solver.**
  Folks who are most successful with the program have a good sense of what problem they're trying to solve.

- **Interact with the data.**
  Most businesses leverage the APIs and the automated data sets more. Small businesses specifically leverage a lot of open data for market sizing and better understanding different neighborhoods and their characteristics.

[Name]

NYC Open Data

[Elevator Pitch]

"We work with more than sixty city agencies in New York to make city data available to the public. We believe that every New Yorker can benefit from Open Data, and Open Data can benefit from every New Yorker."

[Sector]

Multiple

[Description]

In a city as enormous and diffuse as New York, democratizing access to public information so that anyone with a computer can map, analyze and interact with city data is not just a good idea, it's also the law. And for the past seven years, NYC Open Data has been at the forefront of the movement to make public data available to New Yorkers. Formed in 2011 through a collaboration between the Mayor's Office of Data Analytics (MODA) and the Department of Information Technology and Telecommunications (DoITT), NYC Open Data is a mandatory program for New York City's more than sixty city agencies. It's also an amazing resource for entrepreneurs, academics and private citizens alike, allowing them to better understand and support the city they live and work in through data. "Open data isn't just for folks who might be more tech savvy," says Adrienne Schmoeker, director of Civic Engagement and Strategy at MODA. "It's not just for the entrepreneur and startup communities but is also a resource that can be made available and useful to everyone."

Beyond its database of 2,100 data assets – encapsulating everything from demographic data by zip code to an interactive map of subway entrances – NYC Open Data is also a community resource that hosts events like the annual Open Data Week. For startups, early-stage companies and small businesses, NYC Open Data has been used to grow in unique ways. For example, the startup Rentlogic aims to increase transparency in the New York rental market, and it used data from a cross-section of city departments, including the Department of Buildings and the Environmental Control Board, to build its platform. "You might not know what the public will do with the information once you put it out there," Adrienne says, "but you'll always be pleasantly surprised to see the creativity that people bring to the table with the assets that you make public."

[Apply to]

opendata.cityofnewyork.us/engage/

[Links]

Web: opendata.cityofnewyork.us Twitter: @NYCDoITT

- **Come with your milestones and needs.**
  The Future Labs programs are needs- and milestone-oriented; every six months, companies set goals and define what they need to achieve them. Above and beyond all of the other criteria, we have to be able to contribute to the company.

- **Have clear expectations.**
  We expect companies to achieve their milestones; in return, companies can expect us to help them with their needs, whether through our unique and robust university resources, investor and mentor network, or our partner and service provider ecosystem.

- **Contribute to the culture.**
  Besides looking at the typical investment criteria that any investor would look for – things like commercial viability and technical feasibility – we also look for a cultural fit within our space.

- **Be (or become) New York–based.**
  Companies that are accepted and locate at Future Labs are eligible for tax-based incentives through START-UP NY.

[Name]

NYU Tandon Future Labs

[Elevator Pitch] *"We're the first incubator founded with support from New York City. We offer a wide variety of programs that help scale early-stage companies through the startup life cycle."*

[Sector] **Technology (AI, AR, VR), energy efficiency and sustainability, multiple sectors for military veterans**

[Description] NYU Tandon Future Labs provides guidance, resources and community to emerging companies in New York City while encouraging a culture of entrepreneurship. Since its founding in 2009 as the first startup incubator supported by the city through the New York City Economic Development Corporation, Future Labs has grown in scope beyond incubating companies at one location to encompass a wide range of programs and education at four sites strategically spanning the city. These sites comprise the largest university-led startup ecosystem in New York City, serving both non-affiliated founders as well as New York University faculty, students and alumni. Future Labs companies and graduates are valued at $1 billion.

"Around the time of the financial crisis, it was evident that New York City needed to diversify away from dependence upon large corporations in dominant industries such as finance and media," says Steven Kuyan, managing director at Future Labs, "and so we were tasked with creating a process to grow early-stage ventures that had minimal viable products and some capital into companies that were self-sustaining and scalable."

The Future Labs program consists of four hubs: the Urban Future Lab, a leading cleantech and clean energy incubator for emerging companies that are developing solutions for energy efficiency and sustainability; the Digital Future Lab, a hub for the digitalization of industries and technologies such as AR and VR; the Data Future Lab, a hub for AI and data companies; and, the newest addition, the Veterans Future Lab, which supports military veterans, Department of Defense affiliates and their spouses in entrepreneurial ventures. As a New York State Certified Business Incubator, Future Labs also offers companies state resources, and companies located at Future Labs are eligible for tax-based incentives through START-UP NY. The Future Labs program helped launch many of today's leading New York City and global startups such as CB Insights, Clarifai, Honest Buildings and Bounce X.

[Apply to] **futurelabs.nyc**

[Links] Web: **futurelabs.nyc** Facebook: **TheFutureLabs** Twitter: **@NYUFutureLabs**

- **Have a passion for technology.**
  The people who come into Per Scholas have one thing in common: a passion for technology. They're creative problem-solvers who may not have previous experience but they do have a determination to learn and succeed.

- **Meet basic requirements.**
  Students must have a high school diploma or equivalent. They also must pass the TABE test, which assesses adult learners with a tenth-grade reading and math level.

- **Be ready to work hard.**
  Students can expect to spend forty hours per week in the classroom, in addition to three to four hours of homework.

- **Be in and of the community.**
  The greatest thing about Per Scholas classrooms is that they look identical to the communities where we live and work: 90 percent of the student body is diverse, 30 percent of students women and 30 percent are young adults.

[Name]

Per Scholas

[Elevator Pitch]

"We're a national nonprofit that drives positive and proven social change in communities across the country. Through rigorous, tuition-free technology training and professional development, we prepare motivated and curious adults who are unemployed or underemployed for successful careers as IT professionals."

[Sector]

IT support, web development, cybersecurity

[Description]

In the early 1990s, as the emergence of new technologies opened up a new world of opportunities to some, it also created a digital skills divide for others. In New York City, this played out in the education system. "Schools in more affluent communities could afford computers, but schools in communities like the South Bronx weren't able to access the same tech," says Plinio Ayala, president and CEO of Per Scholas. "As a result, an unfair technology skills gap was being created."

Per Scholas was founded in the South Bronx in 1995 with the aim of bridging the digital skills divide. Initially, it did this by employing members of the local community to refurbish donated computers, which were sold or donated back to schools in the Bronx. In 1998, through local employer input, Per Scholas launched an IT Support training course for overlooked communities in New York. Serving a diverse student body, Per Scholas now operates in six cities: New York, NY; Atlanta, GA; Dallas, TX; Cincinnati and Columbus, OH; and the National Capital Region, MD. Course offerings include IT support, web development, cybersecurity, software quality assurance, and data engineering, all of which are taught in an intensive "boot camp" style curriculum coupled with professional development training and all of which are employer informed.

The hard work is worth it. Over 80 percent of graduates are placed in a job and at least 70 percent of placements remain those jobs for at least a year. Platform by Per Scholas, an extension of the model, offers customizable curricula for partner corporations with nuanced jobs that require specific training for in-demand skills. "The learning never stops," Ayala says. "Within tech, there are accessible skills across all industries. If you can get your foot in the door – and it's possible to do that with Per Scholas' entry level courses – and you dedicate yourself to continuing to upskill, that hard work leads to success."

[Apply to]

perscholas.org

[Links]

Web: **perscholas.org** Facebook: **PerScholas** Twitter: **@PerScholas** Instagram: **perscholas**

- **Attend meetups and events to connect with other women in your community.**
  Meeting other women working in technology and innovation in your city is a good way to exchange ideas, talk about challenges in a particular sector and support each other.

- **Download the She Innovates App.**
  Another way to connect and engage with other women is to register for the app, share your experiences and offer advice or mentorship to women who may be starting out their careers.

- **Read up on the Gender Innovation Principles.**
  The principles set the standard for a gender-responsive approach to innovation and provide companies with the benchmark for how to include women throughout the innovation cycle.

- **Sign up to become a She Innovates mentor.**
  Join the Led by HER mentoring program that connects women innovators with mentors who can support and provide advice on how to set-up a startup.

[Name]

She Innovates Global Program

[Elevator Pitch]

"We want to encourage girls and women to play a more important role in the development of innovation in the STEM sectors through mentorship and events as well as building up local communities of women."

[Sector]

Tech, science, innovation

[Description]

The She Innovates Global Program aims to support women working in tech, science and innovation not only in New York but all over the world by providing access to development tools, programs and resources and connecting them to a worldwide network of women innovators. The program provides support in a variety of ways including through a She Innovates app that connects women innovators of all stages in their careers so they can share stories and interact with each other; a series of events and meetups to acquire practical know-how and gain professional support; a She Innovates Award that offers grant funding for women-led solutions that address the specific needs of women and girls; and a mentoring program that links up seasoned professionals with young innovators who are looking for advice in a particular industry.

Women from any background and in all stages of their career are welcome to participate in the array of activities, events, campaigns and programs organized by the program. Women with more professional experience are also encouraged to sign up to become a mentor to help other women develop their skills and abilities.

The She Innovates Global Program is developed by the Global Innovation Coalition for Change (GICC), a partnership between UN Women and leaders from the private sector, academia and nonprofits focused on creating change in the innovation and technology market so women can thrive and reach their potential. Ultimately, the goal of the GICC – which was launched in 2017 – is to empower women and achieve gender equality faster. To date, the GICC already has twenty-seven partners, including Amy Poehler's Smart Girls, MIT Solve, SAP and Sony. In addition to She Innovates and UN Women, GICC is working on a set of Gender Innovation Principles that hope "to provide companies with the benchmark for how to include women through the innovation life cycle" as well as a For Good program that supports women entrepreneurs in South Africa.

[Apply to]

http://www.unwomen.org/en/how-we-work/innovation-and-technology/un-women-global-innovation-coalition-for-change

[Links]

Web: **unwomen.org** Facebook: **unwomen** Twitter: **@un_women** Instagram: **unwomen**

spa

ces

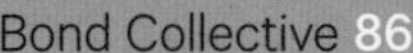

[Name] # Bond Collective

[Address] 55 Broadway, 3rd Floor, New York, NY, 10006

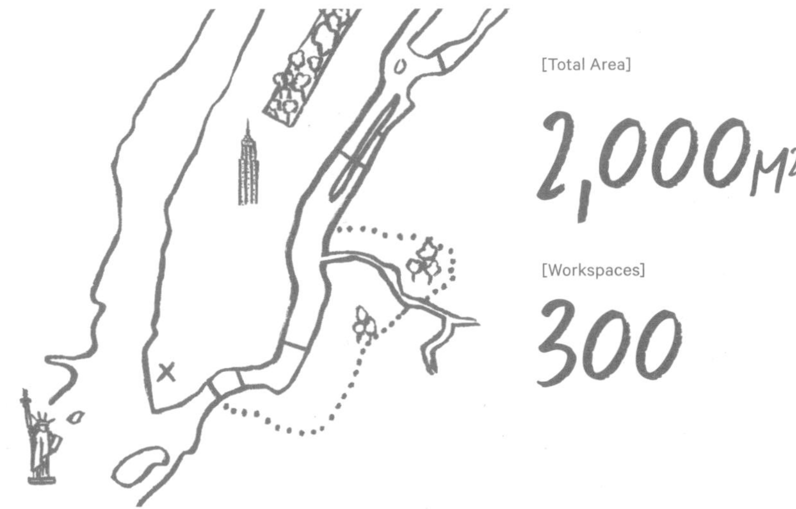

[The Story] Entering into Bond Collective's shared workspace in Manhattan's Financial District is like walking into an entirely new world, one far removed from New York City. It's quiet, clean and artfully decorated, with comfortable blue-suede armchairs, industrial chandeliers, and tasteful embellishments throughout. And most importantly, it's welcoming and friendly. Founded in 2013 by Schlomo Silber and Elie Deitsch, both of whom share a background in construction, Bond Collective operates four shared workspaces across the city, with a fifth soon opening in Bushwick and plans to expand to Washington, DC, and Philadelphia.

For Bond Collective, creating a welcoming community is paramount. Each space is unique and designed to cater to the needs of the community it serves. And as a boutique workspace, the company also places an emphasis on style and sophistication. From themed happy hours to wellness offerings and free breakfasts on Mondays, Bond Collective isn't just an office but a one-stop shop for entrepreneurs, innovators and workers from across multiple industries. "For any startup or anyone who wants to get out of their home and come to a place that's clean, beautiful and respectful, and to be around people who share the same ideals as you, this is the place that you want to be," says Ashley Espinal, Head of Community and Culture at Bond Collective.

[Links] Web: bondcollective.com Facebook: bondcollectiveofficial Twitter: @Bond_Collective

Face of the Space:

Ashley Espinal is the Head of Community and Culture at Bond Collective. With a background in professional dance and operations, Ashley choreographs events, experiences and management at Bond Collective. She started as an assistant manager at 55 Broadway and now oversees all four locations. "I fell in love with the people here," Ashley says. "I really want to be part of a team that values other people and their experiences."

STAY IN TOUCH WITH CIVIC HALL
Twitter: @civichall
Instagram: @civichall
Facebook: @civichallnyc
WiFi: Civic Hall
Password: empathy118
CIVIC HALL

Not Feeling Well
Here is Our First+Aid
First Aid
Plast Bags

[Name]

Civic Hall

[Address] 118 West 22nd Street, 12th Floor, New York, NY 10011

[Total Area]

743M²

[Workspaces]

120

[The Story] Civic Hall is a community space where innovators, entrepreneurs, government employees, hackers, academics, journalists and artists can meet, collaborate and create tools to enhance the relationship between people and government. The space was opened in 2015 by social entrepreneur Andrew Rasiej to house New York City's burgeoning nonprofit startup community. "There are so many tech entrepreneurs in New York City that are interested in making the world a better place, not just making money," says Rasiej, who is also the chairman of the New York Tech Alliance. "They needed a space where they could work alongside like-minded professionals who care about tech for the public good."

Civic Hall is located in a twelfth-floor loft in Manhattan's Flatiron neighborhood. Organizations can pay anywhere from $20 per month for part-time access to $500 per month for full-time access to the space. Civic Hall currently has over one thousand individual members.

Notable alumni include VoteRunLead, a platform that trains women to run for political office, and Heat Seek, a nonprofit that helps impoverished New Yorkers take their landlord to court for not providing enough heat in the winter time.

[Links] Web: **civichall.org** Facebook: **CivicHallNYC** Twitter: **@CivicHall** Instagram: **civichall**

Face of the Space:

Civic Hall founder and CEO Andrew Rasiej is chairman of the New York Tech Alliance, a nonprofit organization that aims to represent, support and lead the New York tech community. Rasiej is also the founder of MOUSE, a youth development nonprofit that provides digital skills training for public school kids in ten states and twenty countries around the world.

SHARE or DIE
drop the ball
DOES IT WORK?
THE RISE OF THE RELUCTANT INNOVATOR KEN BANKS
EVERYTHING IS MISCELLANEOUS DAVID WEINBERGER
A RETURN TO COMMON SENSE
MEDIEVAL EUROPE 400-1500
USED
WHOSE GLOBAL VILLAGE?
THOMAS L. FRIEDMAN Hot, Flat, and Crowded
EVERYTHING IS MISCELLANEOUS DAVID WEINBERGER
PRESIDENTIAL POWER AND THE MODERN PRESIDENTS
KABOOM!
Wunderlich The Secret of Crete
REINVENTING KHOMEINI
David Plouffe
INBOUND MARKETING
Campaign for President
BROAD INFLUENCE
LISA GANSKY the mesh
WHERE EAST EATS WEST
Remaking the Democratic Party
MICROPODER
DYLAN RATIGAN
AMERICA'S MOMENT
GET OUT THE VOTE
perfect enemies
CHRISTINE TODD WHITMAN IT'S MY PARTY TOO
THE SOCIAL LIFE OF INFORMATION
CREATIVE STRATEGY Generation
CLIVE THOMPSON SMARTER THAN YOU THINK
THE WAR ON LEAKERS

[Name]

New Lab

[Address] 19 Morris Avenue, Building 128, Cumberland Gate, Brooklyn, NY 11205

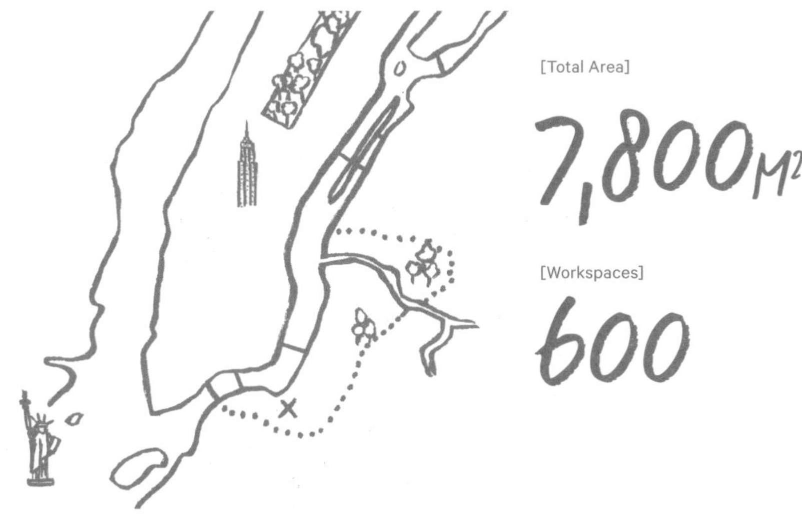

[The Story]

When New Lab cofounder and CEO David Belt first walked into Brooklyn Navy Yard Building 128, he was immediately taken by it. It was not only the eighty-foot ceilings and fascinating history but also the possibility of restoring this empty turn-of-the-century ship-building factory to both bring manufacturing back into the heart of New York City and steer it boldly into the future. "It was one of the most incredibly dramatic spaces I'd seen in New York, and I'm in the business of looking at dramatic spaces," Belt says of the building, which is now home to over one hundred emerging technology startups working across multiple disciplines, including robotics, IoT, AI, blockchain, agtech and clean energy.

Working with the Navy Yard, the City of New York, and his business partner Scott Cohen, Belt founded New Lab in 2016, transforming the space into a platform for entrepreneurs, enterprise partners, policy makers and investors. It features over $3.5 million of prototyping equipment, including 3D printing, CNC shops, and electronics benches, as well as a cafe, living rooms and communal meeting spaces. "We want to be a signifier of optimism in technology in New York," Belt says. "If you want to do a new idea, you have to do it in an old building, because it gives gravitas – it grounds the people who work here."

[Links] Web: **newlab.com** Facebook: **NewLabNavyYard** Twitter: **@NewLab** Instagram: **newlab**

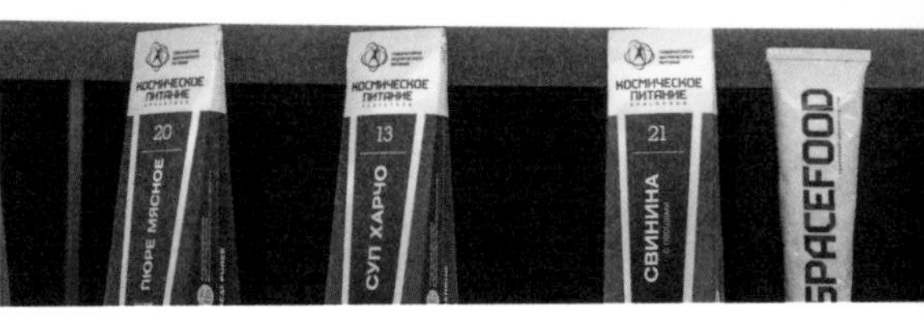

Face of the Space:

David Belt is a leader in creative real estate development, working on some of the city's most innovative spaces, including Saint Ann's Warehouse, a converted theater in Brooklyn. Belt has executed over $1 billion in private and institutional development projects worldwide, collaborating with businesses, foundations, and individuals. He's also a self-professed optimist who is, in his own words, "incredibly fascinated with what's going on with technology right now."

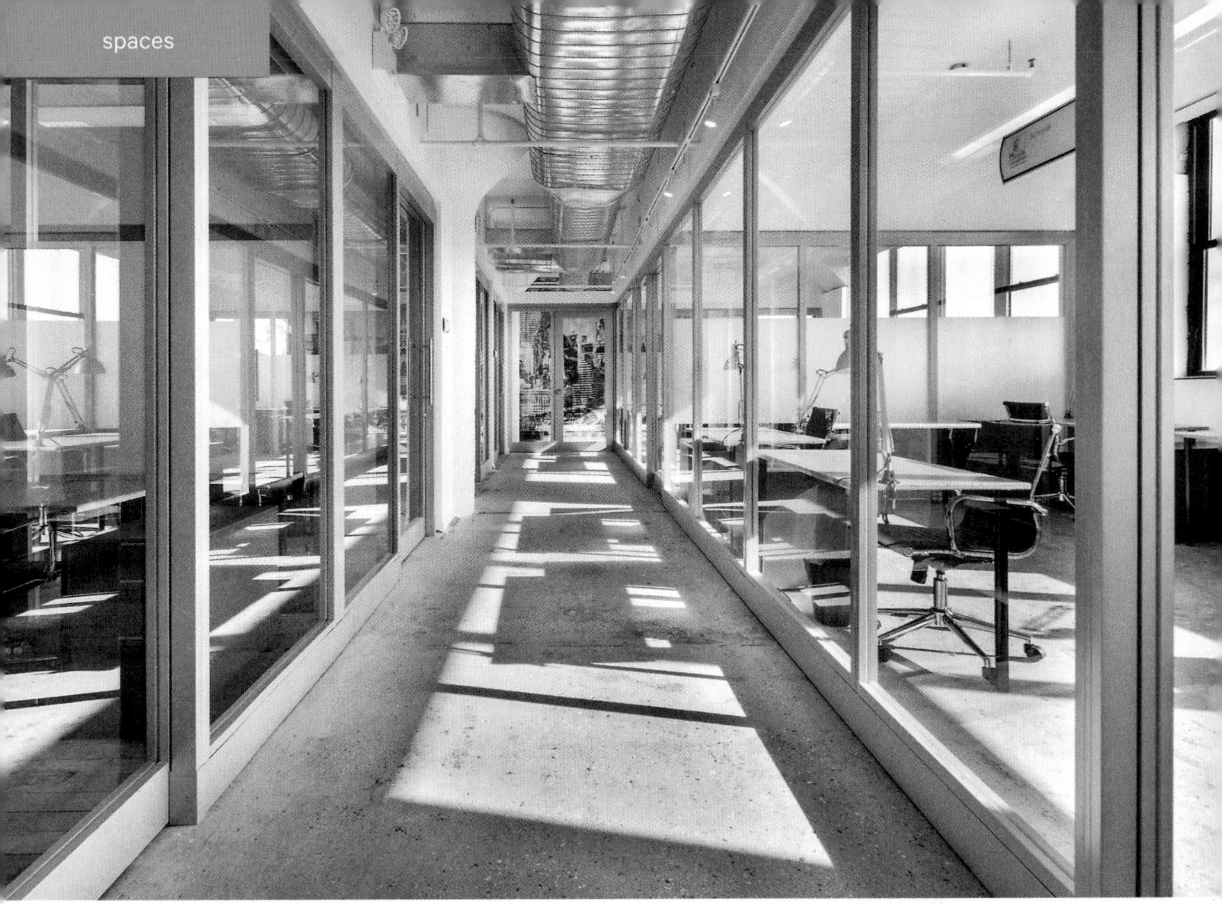

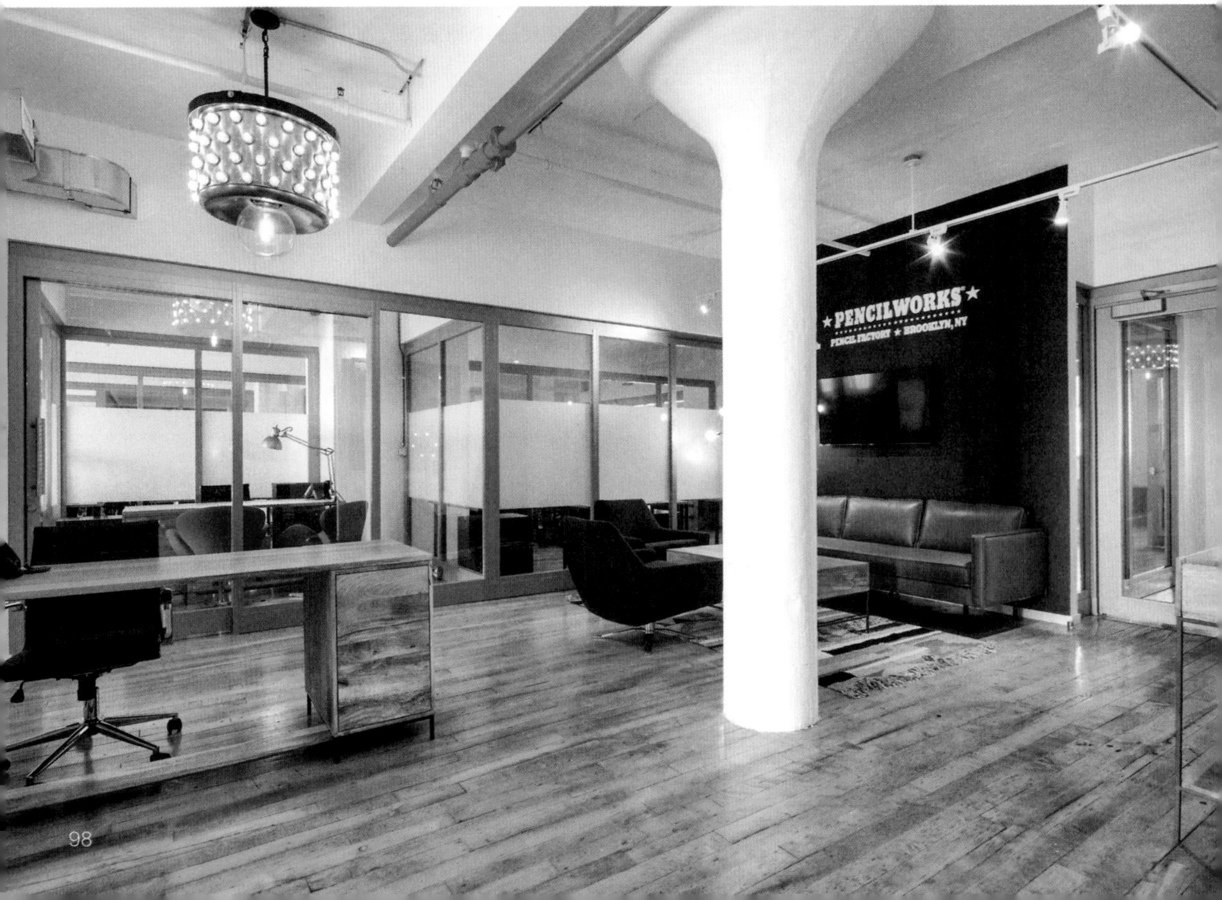
★PENCILWORKS★
PENCIL FACTORY ★ BROOKLYN, NY

[Name]
PencilWorks

[Address] 61 Greenpoint Avenue, 6th Floor, Brooklyn, New York 11222

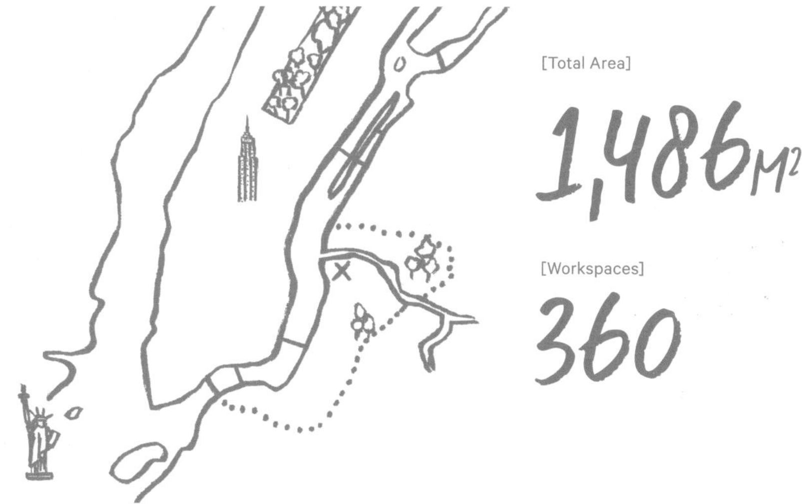

[Total Area]

1,486 M2

[Workspaces]

360

[The Story] PencilWorks is cultivating a dynamic, creative and collaborative community for Brooklyn's nomadic workforce. The coworking space is located inside the former factory of the Eberhard Faber Pencil Company. The reinforced-concrete, Art Deco–style factory building was erected in 1923 as the largest structure in the Greenpoint manufacturing district. Today, the Pencil Factory, as the building is known, houses six floors of makers and creators of all types, with PencilWorks located on the top floor. Pencil Factory owner Scott Berger started PencilWorks because he believes in nurturing and supporting businesses as a way of fostering a diverse community. "Our community is really collaborative," says Nathan Windsor, community developer at PencilWorks. "We host a variety of businesses, including advisory consulting companies, VC startups in retail, exponential technologies, arts, fashion and media. Everyone comes here to be inspired, collaborate and do their best work."

Opened in 2016, PencilWorks features a minimalist design and lots of natural light. There are fourteen private desks, forty-nine office spaces (ranging in size up to twenty-person capacity), and three conference rooms that can accommodate up to fifteen. There's also lounge space, a coffee and espresso bar, weekly networking and community events, a bike-sharing program and access to VR and AR technology. In addition, members receive discounts at local Greenpoint businesses. Pricing ranges from $12.95 per day for access to the coworking space to $995 per month for an office. PencilWorks accepts a variety of cryptocurrencies for rent payments.

[Links] Web: **pencilwork.com** Facebook: **PencilWorksBK** Twitter: **@PencilWorksBK**

Face of the Space:
Scott Berger is a New York native who has spent most of his career working in global hardware distribution. He attended Boston University and Cardozo Law School at Yeshiva University. Scott's family bought the Pencil Factory in 1978, and Scott runs the facility along with his brother David.

THE GLOBAL GOALS
Millions of women all over the globe are experiencing some sort of gender inequality. Through initiatives enabled by technology, progress is being made in all aspects of women's lives – including the area of economic and business empowerment.
World leaders have committed to achieving the United Nations 17 Sustainable Development Goals (SDGs), but they won't succeed alone.
The largest garbage dumps in the world are underwater. An estimated 8 million tons of plastic is added to them every year, even though they are located in the middle of our oceans.
4 QUALITY EDUCATION
5 GENDER EQUALITY
17 PARTNERSHIPS FOR THE GOALS
14 LIFE BELOW WATER
How SAP is helping
WRIGHT

[Name]

SAP Next-Gen

[Address] 10 Hudson Yards, 48th Floor, New York, NY, 10001

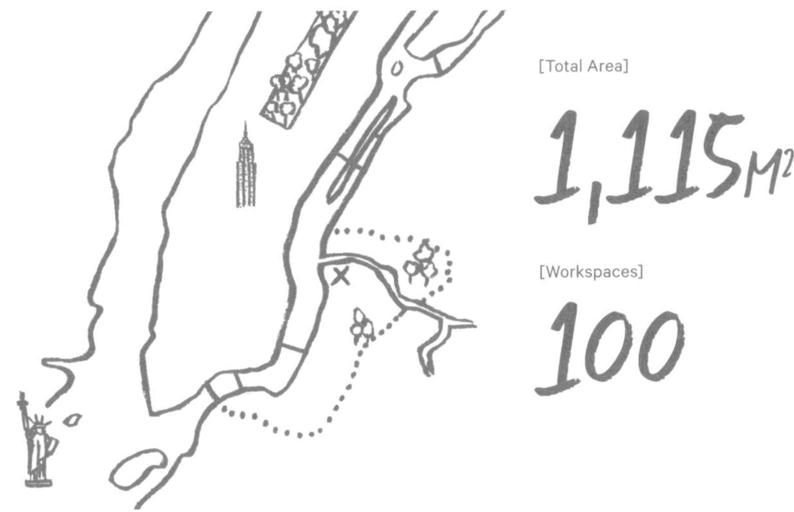

[The Story]

As soon as you step onto the 48th floor of 10 Hudson Yards, you feel the energy. The space hums with a palpable excitement that seems to burst from New York City itself. SAP Next-Gen floats above the city, encased in floor-to-ceiling glass windows and offering awe-inspiring views. The space, which is linked to SAP's global innovation network, is airy, open, and has the feel of an innovation garage. It's all about bringing together everyone from corporations to academic thought leaders, researchers, students, startups, accelerators, tech partners, purpose-driven partners, venture firms, futurists and SAP experts. More specifically, it's SAP Next-Gen's flagship location for driving innovation with purpose based on the UN Global Goals for Sustainable Development.

This open-mindedness is shown equally through its innovative offerings, which range from creative boot camps on new mindsets to innovation tours featuring SAP's latest technologies as well as connections to the New York startup and tech communities, and a meetup scene that brings together purpose-driven citizens from across New York. "With science-fiction thinking, purpose thinking and exponential technologies across twenty-five industries, we inspire companies to think big and without boundaries, and to link innovation to purpose," says Ben Christensen, global innovation manager at SAP Next-Gen and science-fiction community lead.

[Links] Web: **sap.com/next-gen** Facebook: **SAPNextGen** Twitter: **@SAPNextGen** Instagram: **sapnextgen**

SAP Next-Gen in New York has everything: responsive robots, a coffee bar, musical instruments, VR equipment, a photo wall and more. And it's home to the Hasso Plattner Institute in New York, as well as an incubator for women-owned businesses called the SAP.iO Foundry.

"Humans can only be as creative as the circumstances or the space that you put them in," says Sandra Moerch, site manager of SAP Next-Gen in New York and global head of the SAP Next-Gen brand. "That's the design spirit behind this space." Almost anyone across industries and age groups – from students to accelerators to startups to corporations – can get involved with SAP Next-Gen, as long as they're committed to pushing the boundaries of technology for social good.

[Name]
The Assemblage

[Address] NoMad House, 114 East 25th Street, New York, NY 10015

[Total Area]

4,459 M²

[Workspaces]

350

[The Story] The Assemblage is a coworking space with special offerings like yoga, meditation and ayurvedic foods aimed at helping members ignite consciousness and collaboration. The idea for The Assemblage came to founder Rodrigo Nino while he was hallucinating on ayahuasca in Peru. "What I saw is that we're living in a society where all our actions and ideas are based on our own self-interest and not the collective well-being," said Rodrigo, who sought out ayahuasca to help cope with his anxiety after being diagnosed with melanoma. "I realized we needed to assemble that complex through a community of like-minded individuals."

Rodrigo, a real estate developer by trade, raised over $500 million for his coworking space through investments from thirty-four different countries. The Assemblage NoMad location is 48,000 square feet stretched across twelve floors. It features lounges, private and shared workspaces, conference rooms, meditation environments, private event spaces and a screening room. There's also a rooftop terrace, a library, an alchemy bar and an ayurvedic plant-based cafe. The space features lots of greenery and woven textiles created by the Shipbo Tribe of the Amazon, as well as a curated selection of artwork by community members. In addition to NoMad House, The Assemblage has a second location on 17 John Street in Manhattan's Financial District.

[Links] Web: **theassemblage.com** Facebook: **TheAssemblageNYC** Twitter: **@AssemblageNYC**

Face of the Space:
Rodrigo Nino is a Colombian native and founder of Prodigy Network, a platform that uses crowdfunding to buy commercial real estate. Nino believes that crowdfunding will democratize commercial real estate by providing a new asset class for individuals. Nino has spoken at worldwide conferences and has been a noteworthy guest at NYU, MIT, Yale, Harvard University and the AEDES gallery in Berlin.

KUSMI TEA

[Name]
The Yard

[Address] 33 West 60th Street, New York, NY 10023

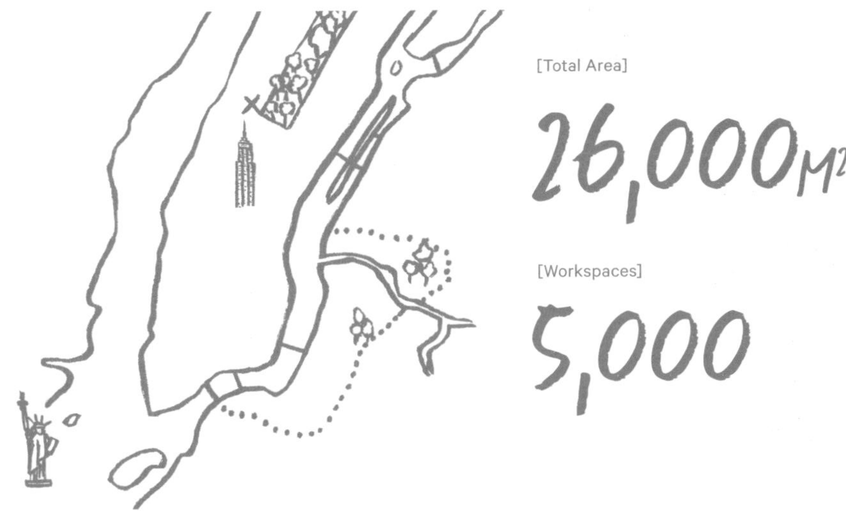

[Total Area] 26,000 M2

[Workspaces] 5,000

[The Story] Between getting ready for band practice and taking care of his six kids running about the house, Morris Levy, cofounder and CEO of The Yard, needed more than a home office. "The kids came home at four-thirty, and my work day was over," Morris says. But when he perused the market for offices, he was disappointed, so he decided to take matters into his own hands. Only three weeks later, Morris and his business partner, Richard Beyda, had secured their first building: a former industrial space in Williamsburg with high ceilings and wide columns. Within six months, the space was full of members growing their businesses. Eight years later, The Yard is operating coworking spaces out of New York, Boston, Washington, DC, and Philadelphia.

The Yard's midtown location features exposed brick and natural light, as well as greenery, colorful art and tasteful decorations throughout. This is typical of The Yard's spaces, which aim to be not just a coworking space but also neighborhood fixtures. "We saw what bringing three hundred people to one block does for local businesses," Morris says. "People are in restaurants, they're buying from bodegas, they're going to the bar. Before we open, we reach out to local businesses in each neighborhood to form alliances, discounts, and perks for our members."

[Links] Web: **theyard.com** Facebook: **workattheyard** Twitter: **@WorkAtTheYard** Instagram: **theyard**

Face of the Space:
Morris Levy, CEO and cofounder of The Yard, has a background in real-estate development with an additional fifteen years of experience in the fashion and apparel industry. A Brooklyn native, Morris took evening classes in real estate and finance at NYU before managing a portfolio of industrial and commercial properties. He lives in Brooklyn with his wife and six kids.

THE
YARD
SPACE TO WORK
ALTO

WELCOME
GUESTS
PLEASE SIGN IN HERE
EXIT
SMART
TIES

[Name]

Urban Tech Hub at Company

[Address] 335 Madison Avenue, Floor 4, New York, NY 10017

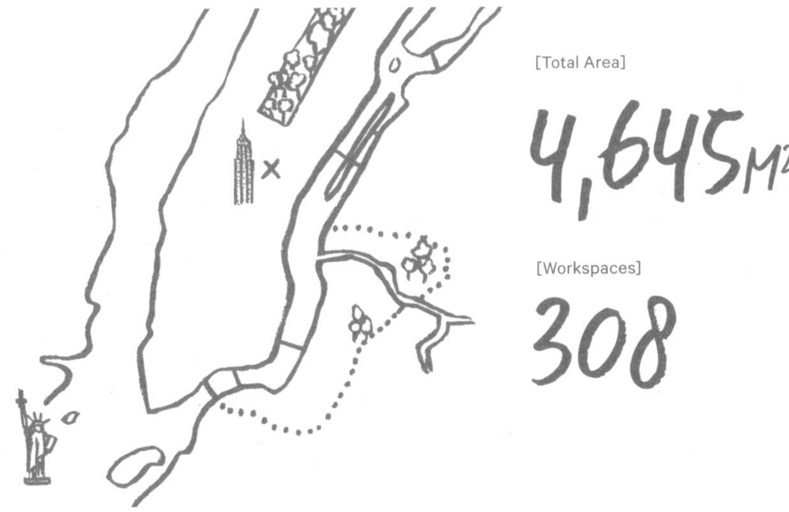

[Total Area]

4,645 M2

[Workspaces]

308

[The Story]

Urban Tech Hub at Company is an office space inhabited by post-accelerator tech startups focused on solving the challenges of modern urban living. Venture platform Grand Central Tech (now operated by Company) founded Urban Tech Hub in conjunction with New York City in 2016 as a way to help the city capitalize on technological innovations, especially in the face of climate change. "We're creating an ecosystem of like-minded businesses," says Robinson Hernandez, executive director of Urban Tech Hub. "People focused on making positive changes in the world come here because it's a fun and collaborative environment."

Urban Tech Hub occupies fifty thousand square feet inside the former Biltmore Hotel, a 105-year-old structure that was renovated into an office space in 1981. Inside are twelve office spaces of varying sizes, the largest of which can accommodate up to fifty people, along with an open area with seventy-eight additional desks. The space offers an open, minimalist design that encourages collaboration. There's a curated selection of urban-oriented art and lounge spaces for a more casual work environment. Company has plans to expand the space to over 250,000 square feet, with additional amenities such as a library, fitness center (with pool) and outdoor terrace. "We're becoming a tech campus that can provide amenities similar to what you'd find in Silicon Valley," Robinson says.

[Links] Web: **hubatgct.com** Facebook: **GrandCentralTech** Twitter: **@GCTech**

Face of the Space:

Robinson Hernandez, executive director of Urban Tech Hub, has dedicated his career to finding ways to streamline the regulatory environment to help governments operate more efficiently. A Queens native, Robinson attended Boston College as an undergrad and New York University for a Master of Urban Planning degree. He's worked at General Electric, Ernst & Young and for the City of New York, and was part of GovWorks.com during the initial dotcom wave. He joined Company in 2016 to help launch Urban Tech Hub.

[Name]
WeWork

[Address] 115 West 18th Street, New York, NY 10011

[Total desks in NYC]

56,257

[Workspaces]

1,172

[The Story] There's a reason WeWork has grown from one location in SoHo to three hundred spaces and 250,000 global members in eight years. WeWork is more than a space; it's a community. This is reflected in everything from its membership offerings to its architecture. It has glass walls and windows throughout with open common areas, communal tables, and fridges and cupboards stocked with drinks and snacks. The space is designed to encourage cross-pollination between entrepreneurs, small businesses and enterprise employees. "What we used to consider office space is nothing like it is today," says Rui Barros, head of operations for US/Canada East. "The workforce is looking for a comfortable environment that enables innovation and creativity."

Founded in 2010 by Adam Neumann and Miguel McKelvey, the idea behind WeWork was to create a space where individuals could tackle challenges together in a collaborative environment. And that mission continues to live on as the company evolves, adding other capacities like Powered by We, a product for larger companies to build their own spaces using the WeWork framework; and Global Access, which allows workers to go to any WeWork space in seventy cities and twenty-two countries. "We're continuing to find ways to evolve our brand and our offerings," Rui says. "It's pretty mind-blowing how far we've come."

[Links] Web: **wework.com** Facebook: **WeWork** Twitter: **@wework** Instagram: **wework**

Face of the Space:

Rui Barros came to WeWork after nearly two decades of experience in the hospitality industry. Now in charge of running the US and Canada East Region for WeWork, including the tristate market – New York, New Jersey, and Connecticut – Rui is continually impressed with WeWork's commitment to its values. "The company is true to its mission, and it's laser-focused on delivering that value," he says. "Day in and day out, it's an exciting place to be."

exp

erts

In partnership with:

Dan Levitan / BerlinRosen

Senior Vice President

Startups often hear they need PR without understanding what it is, why they need it, or even how it can impact their business. "Entrepreneurs sometimes feel like they need to generate buzz because that's what they've been told or they've seen a more established competitor getting press around a product," says Dan Levitan, senior vice president of BerlinRosen, a full-service public relations agency with a team of 130 people spread across New York, Washington, DC and Los Angeles. "But as a young company, it's important to be judicious about resources, understand what you're getting for your investment, and define how PR can help you achieve your business goals."

So, what exactly is PR and how can it play a role in a startup's growth? Dan, who leads BerlinRosen's tech practice, says it's about talking to the public in a strategic way and communicating a unique message to specific audiences. This can be done in a multitude of ways, including through traditional media, direct marketing, social media or creative stunts. Depending on a startup's stage, industry and strategy, PR can influence a business in different ways. For startups looking to develop or launch their first product or service, it can help create initial awareness about the company and support early customer acquisition goals. But PR can also help startups find investors, partners or potential employees. "The crucial thing is to make sure your PR plan is calibrated to what your business really needs," says Dan.

When it comes to press releases, there are strong and mixed opinions on their importance in the startup world. Some companies swear by them, while some prominent tech journalists say startups don't need them. "It's often worth doing press releases, especially for startups, if only to go through the exercise of trying to tell a clear story and articulate the news you want to announce," says Dan. "At the end of the process, you'll have a document that can live on as people search for you or come across your company. But on its own, it's not going to replace proactively reaching out to reporters, understanding what they want to cover, and working with them to get a story that supports your message."

Most important tips for startups:

- **Define how you'd like PR to help achieve your business goals.** Whether it's acquiring new customers, creating company awareness in a new market or attracting investors, the first step in developing a PR strategy is to outline what you want to achieve with it.

- **Don't pitch your product or service until it's in tip-top shape.** You've got only one shot to impress reporters with a new product. Wait until your product or service is nearly perfect and has a good user experience. Otherwise, you'll need to persuade them to try it again, which won't be easy.

- **Build and maintain relationships with journalists.** Even before you have any news to announce, it's valuable to start connecting with the press on social media or in real life. Relationships are key in the media business.

If you decide to write a press release as part of your media relations strategy, one thing to remember is that reporters and editors are super busy. This means you need to be clear about what the news is; be concise about what makes your product, service or company different; and get to your main points as quickly as possible. Another thing that helps is reading news related to your business. This will give you a better sense of what journalists are covering in that realm, how they're writing about it, and topics they might be interested in.

For startups still iterating on their product, Dan has some words of caution: "Don't pitch your product or service to reporters asking to try it firsthand until it's nearly perfect and you're really proud of it. Reporters are probably only going to try it once, and they'll decide within a couple of minutes whether they're interested in writing about it. If you don't have a great user experience off the bat, you're likely not ready to be asking for a review." It's smarter to leave a good first impression rather than going back to journalists several months later and persuading them to try something again. Chances are they won't have the time or interest.

"Media is a relationships business," says Dan, "and any relationships you develop with reporters will continue to pay off down the line, even as they go on to cover different beats and write for different outlets." If you don't have an announcement in the foreseeable future, it's still worth developing relationships with reporters who cover your industry. It's a chance to explain your business, establish your credentials and become an expert source, and it will lead to better coverage down the line.

About

BerlinRosen is a leading strategic public relations and communications firm delivering high-impact media relations, digital strategy and creative services to clients ranging from global technology leaders to early-stage companies. As campaigners and integrated communications professionals, the team knows where there are opportunities to break through and what it takes to move the needle. Whether startups want to raise their profile, generate buzz on a new product or solution, reach out to people in a specific market, communicate in a crisis, or persuade consumers, BerlinRosen can help.

[Contact] Email: info@berlinrosen.com

[Links] Web: berlinrosen.com Facebook: berlinrosen Twitter: @BerlinRosen

“Media is a relationships business, and any relationships you develop with reporters will continue to pay off down the line.”

Adrien Colombié / Flying Saucer Studio

Founder and Creative Director

It makes no difference how great your product, service or company is if you can't clearly communicate to people what it is, why it matters and what the benefits are. "Many startups spend so much of their time on the product, developing features and technical aspects, that they forget how important it is to take the time to craft a story around the product, highlight its benefits and build the overall brand," says Adrien Colombié, founder and creative director of Flying Saucer Studio, a design and branding studio that works with startups of all stripes and all sizes. Although the company is based in New York and Paris, its creative team works mostly remotely from around the world.

After getting a taste of the startup world through his role as mentor at Techstars, Adrien decided to leave his advertising career behind in favor of working more with passionate entrepreneurs. In 2016, he founded Flying Saucer Studio to empower startups with creative design and marketing strategies. "Branding is much bigger than a logo and the colors you use," he says. "A logo is just an asset, but a brand is defined by a company's story, voice, personality, visual elements and content. It's much more complex, and it's about creating an emotional connection. It's a toolbox you can use every day, both internally and externally."

Having worked with startups from various stages and industries, Adrien has a couple pieces of advice for entrepreneurs trying to navigate the realm of branding. First, he adamantly believes that people will only take you as seriously as you tell them to. "Your first, second and twenty-fifth impressions matter: you need to invest in consistency and a well-built brand, and you need to dress to impress. says Adrien, "As the old saying goes, 'Dress for the job you want, not the one you have.'" Building a brand is about building trust, and an element of that is looking the part.

Oftentimes, a startup will have a big vision and want to go from zero to a hundred immediately, but Adrien advises to take things step by step: "Instead of trying to conquer the world at once with a complete and complex overhaul – which is often difficult and expensive – start small or go for a niche market. Try things, test them, improve them, and then scale."

Most important tips for startups:

- **People will only take you as seriously as you tell them to.** That means every impression you make counts, so make sure your brand is consistent, well built and well presented. As the saying goes, "Dress for the job you want, not the one you have."

- **Start small and iterate fast.** Failure is going to happen – it's simply part of the process – so it's rarely the right move to invest in a complete, complex and expensive overhaul right off the bat. Try things, test them, improve them, and then scale.

- **Be clear and honest about where you stand.** Take stock of where your company stands, including its short-, medium- and long-term goals; its financial restrictions; and its available brainpower. Only then can you start working backwards from those realistic and achievable goals.

Another thing to pay attention to are the details. The little things matter – a lot – and especially when it comes to building up a brand for a fledgling startup. Pay close attention to your gut and zoom in on anything that trips you up, rubs you the wrong way or catches your eye; these details can help you define the contours of your product, mission and story.

It's also crucial to take a good, hard look at the company and take stock of where it's at. Where does your company stand right now? What's feasible? What's your budget? What are your goals in the next five years? In the next ten years? Only then can you start working backwards from those realistic and achievable goals. "A central part of our approach is to meet people where they are, wherever that may be," says Adrien.

In addition to offering branding services, Flying Saucer Studio also helps startups create customized campaigns that combine digital design, UX/UI design and video direction as well as marketing and SEM strategies.

Final words of wisdom? "Never get too comfortable," says Adrien. "No matter the size of your brand or the success of your most recent marketing coup, it's important to keep in mind that companies are living, evolving things; their stories and branding need to reflect that growth."

About

Flying Saucer Studio is a fully remote design studio backed by a team of five-star creatives spread all over the world. The team fuses its digital design, UX, UI and branding skills with advanced marketing and SEM knowledge in order to create powerful, tailor-made campaigns that convert. Flying Saucer Studio is based in New York and Paris.

[Contact] Email: adrien@flyingsaucer.nyc

[Links] Web: flyingsaucer.nyc Instagram: flyingsaucerstudio LinkedIn: company/flying-saucer-studio

"A logo is just an asset, but a brand is defined by a company's story, voice, personality, visual elements and content. It's much more complex, and it's about creating an emotional connection."

Heather Corcoran / Kickstarter

Design & Technology Outreach Lead

It's no surprise that more and more entrepreneurs and startups are looking to crowdfunding to finance a project. When done right, it can not only help raise money but also build up a community of early adopters and enthusiastic supporters to get an idea off the ground. Heather Corcoran, Design and Technology Outreach Lead at Kickstarter, says, "Inviting people in to get involved and have a front-row seat in your process as you bring something to life can deepen your connection with them."

As one of the earliest crowdfunding platforms on the scene, Kickstarter has helped projects such as the Pebble smartwatch and Oculus Rift headset build a fanbase, garner attention and attract more funding and collaborators down the line. Heather, who has been working at Kickstarter for the past two years, has some tips for those interested in dipping their toes into this mode of financing and launching their own Kickstarter campaign.

First, believe in your idea. It sounds so simple, and yet at one time or another, we've probably heard about or stumbled across an interesting project with lackluster communications that failed to meet its financial goal. "It's really important to pick the right project, because this is something you're going to be spending a lot of time on," she says. "Be able to express your idea and vision with enthusiasm."

A big part of connecting to potential backers is being able to spark interest and tell a good story about your project. There are many ways to do this, and much of it has to do with building a sense of trust with your audience. "When people know how something is made – when they know the person behind it or the context it's coming from – they're more likely to get involved with the project," says Heather. "It can become more meaningful to backers." After clearly communicating the who, what, where, why, when and how on your project page, there's also room to enhance your storytelling by adding a video or imagery to identify core features.

One thing to keep in mind during this phase? "Make sure the tone of your Kickstarter project page matches the scale of your ambition," she advises, "It's about giving people a sense of confidence that you can deliver the projects you're promising." This means, if you're developing a complex product and thinking of manufacturing it at scale, you should have a well-produced film

Most important tips for startups:

- **Choose a project you're passionate about and ready to invest some time into.** If you don't believe in your idea, no one else will either.

- **Tell a compelling narrative about you and your project to spark interest and connect with your audience on a deeper level.** Start with the who, what, where, why, when and how, and don't forget about using images and video to enhance your storytelling.

- **Make sure the tone of your Kickstarter project page matches the scale of your ambition.**
  If you're developing a complex product and want to manufacture it at scale, you should have a well-produced film and photos to match; but if you're working on a DIY project, then it makes sense for your video and images to also have a DIY aesthetic.

and photos to complement the campaign; but if you're working on a DIY electronic project, then it makes sense for your video and images to also have a crafty DIY aesthetic.

Since authenticity and transparency are key elements in leading a successful Kickstarter campaign, Heather had some thoughts about how to approach this: "At the outset, it's not just about communicating the exciting and innovating aspects of your project; it's also about being clear about what your challenges are and how you're going to overcome them. It's okay to be honest about the fact that you might not know how to solve the challenges in front of you." After all, people are often more sympathetic than we think, especially if they know you're being transparent with them. Having a better understanding of the ups and downs of how something is made might even lead to deepening the sense of connection between the maker and the backer.

To learn more about starting a project on Kickstarter, check out the Kickstarter website for more resources and keep your eyes out for events at its NYC headquarters. Recently, Kickstarter also launched Hardware Studio – an initiative geared towards hardware creators – alongside the manufacturing experts at Avnet and Dragon Innovation.

About

Kickstarter helps artists, musicians, filmmakers, designers and other creators find the resources and support they need to make their ideas a reality. To date, tens of thousands of creative projects – big and small – have come to life with the support of the Kickstarter community. In 2015, Kickstarter became a Benefit Corporation, which are for-profit companies obligated to consider the impact of their decisions on society, not only on shareholders.

[Contact] Email: **kickstarter.com/contact**

[Links] Web: **kickstarter.com** Facebook: **Kickstarter** Twitter: **@kickstarter** Instagram: **kickstarter**

"Inviting people in to get involved and have a front-row seat in your process as you bring something to life can deepen your connection with them."

Ann Rosenberg / SAP Next-Gen

Senior Vice President and Global Head of SAP Next-Gen

When it comes to startups and corporations, each has what the other wants: startups are agile, innovative and experimental, while corporations are filled with experienced leaders, have expansive networks, and are equipped with plentiful resources. Together, they have the potential to leave a positive mark on the world. Although startups and corporations are often perceived as polar opposites, it's becoming increasingly clear that collaborations between the two can propel impactful ideas forward in a mutually beneficial way. "Many startups think that getting venture capital is the only way to be successful, but they don't realize that there are so many new collaboration models now that didn't exist before," says Ann Rosenberg, senior vice president and global head of SAP Next-Gen.

Accelerator programs, matchmaking services and corporate innovation initiatives are now bringing startups and corporations closer than ever before. Ann believes this is a great opportunity to explore different ways of combining classic business models, startup mindsets and purpose-driven issues together, especially those linked with the United Nations' seventeen Global Goals, which SAP is committed to supporting. From eliminating poverty and hunger, to striving for gender equality and cleaner energy, the UN Global Goals aim to build a healthier planet, improve billions of lives around the world and achieve a sustainable future.

Once entrepreneurs are in touch with corporations that might be able to help them access new customers and scale their startups, a big issue they often run into is not knowing how to talk to corporates. Startups might know how to pitch a VC or an audience at a conference, but when it comes to chatting up corporates, they can fall flat. "Working with a corporation is another ball game. It can be a long process where you need to bring your pitch forward many times," explains Ann. "It's different from talking to a VC, so you should research the corporation, understand their needs and tailor your pitch accordingly."

A good thing to remember is that many corporations often work with management-consultant companies, so they're used to getting a lot of external presentations. Given this, Ann suggests focusing less on how great your idea is and more on how your startup can come in and solve a problem or issue, or create a new opportunity for them in a market.

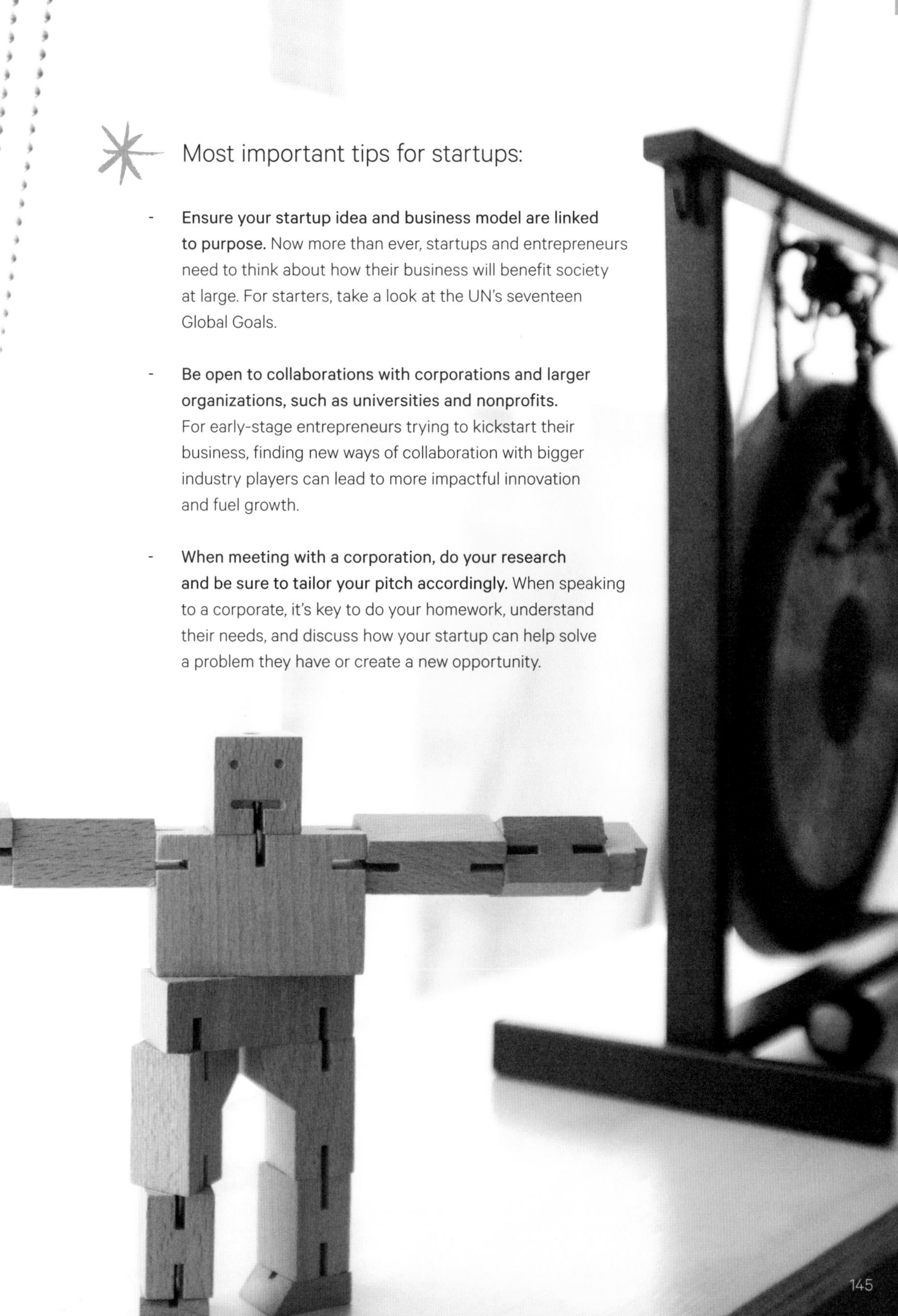

Most important tips for startups:

- **Ensure your startup idea and business model are linked to purpose.** Now more than ever, startups and entrepreneurs need to think about how their business will benefit society at large. For starters, take a look at the UN's seventeen Global Goals.

- **Be open to collaborations with corporations and larger organizations, such as universities and nonprofits.** For early-stage entrepreneurs trying to kickstart their business, finding new ways of collaboration with bigger industry players can lead to more impactful innovation and fuel growth.

- **When meeting with a corporation, do your research and be sure to tailor your pitch accordingly.** When speaking to a corporate, it's key to do your homework, understand their needs, and discuss how your startup can help solve a problem they have or create a new opportunity.

The SAP Next-Gen program expanded its footprint to New York City in 2017 by opening an innovation space on the forty-eighth floor at 10 Hudson Yards, in partnership with the Hasso Plattner Institute. "New York is not only a city but an international stage that inspires the world," says Ann. "The city attracts C-level executives and board members from all over the world, and the UN is also headquartered here. There's so much diversity in terms of people, cultures and industries – it's the perfect place to position your startup."

The aim of SAP Next-Gen is to connect participating startups and companies with SAP's network of academic institutions, startups, corporations, purpose-driven organizations and SAP customers, as well as partners in New York City and around the globe, to accelerate innovation linked to the UN Global Goals. In the Big Apple, SAP Next-Gen hosts innovation tours, informal meetups, boot camps and industry summits, among other initiatives. It also offers a startup matchmaker program that links entrepreneurs to SAP customers and corporates in specific industries.

"The thing about technology today is that you can do anything you want with it," says Ann. "And when you can do anything, you really need to figure out what you most want to do and why. There's a risk that some ideas are simply not ambitious enough, and that's why we use science-fiction thinking to open up entirely new horizons on what is possible, and the 17 UN Global Goals as a framework to align innovation with purposeful outcomes. " Due to our current societal landscape, now more than ever, entrepreneurs need to consider the implications of the businesses they're creating with technology, redefine what it means to have a successful startup, and innovate with purpose.

About

SAP Next-Gen is a purpose-driven innovation university and community aligned with SAP's commitment to the UN's seventeen Global Goals for sustainable development. SAP Next-Gen in New York connects the diverse perspectives of next-generation innovators in New York to SAP's global innovation and development ecosystem. Its goal is to reimagine the future of industries and of the intelligent enterprise, seed disruptive innovation with startups, and build skills for digital futures.

[Contact] Email: ann.rosenberg@sap.com

[Links] Web: sap.com/next-gen Facebook: SAPNextGen Twitter: @SAPNextGen Instagram: sapnextgen

“Many startups don’t realize that there are so many new collaboration models now that didn’t exist before.”

foun

ders

Brian Frumberg

CEO and Founder / VentureOut

Brian Frumberg was working at a venture capital fund when he happened upon an unspoken norm: almost no American early-stage investors were putting their money into foreign companies. After extensive research on why this was the case, he started teaching post-seed founders from abroad how to attract American investors, clients and customers in programs run by his company, VentureOut. Eventually, he extended VentureOut's programs to a dozen specific sectors, regardless of country. Twenty percent of participants are now from the US. Over the last five years, VentureOut has worked with 850 companies from 25 countries. According to Brian, collectively VentureOut alumni have now raised over $1 billion.

What did you do before founding VentureOut?

When I was in high school in the late 90s, I got to intern at a number of "dot-coms. " After a misguided focus on finance, and the travails of the financial crisis, I found myself back in tech, eventually at a venture capital fund, Gotham Ventures, my last job before VentureOut.

How did you find out that foreign startups needed help in New York?

I was at Gotham Ventures and had the opportunity to go to a networking lunch. There, I met someone who worked in innovation at the Canadian Consulate who was trying to figure out how to attract New York venture capitalists to Canadian companies. I followed up and said I'd be happy to work with them to solve that problem. I came up with a proposal to run short intensive programs two to four times a year in which the government of Canada could find the best companies there and showcase them to the VC community in New York City. My thought was that if you did this for two to three years, people would start associating the brand of Canada with venture-backed businesses, and it would be easier to get investors.

The day before we were to sign a contract and begin work on this project, the Canadian government clawed back all unused budget from consulates around the world as a result of challenges stemming from the financial crisis. Left with a great plan and no partner, I had a thought, if Canada – so close geographically to the US, with porous borders, the same language, similar culture and a great tech ecosystem and universities – had trouble getting US venture capitalists to pay attention to their startups, then the rest of the world must be totally f*#ked!

Brian Frumberg / VentureOut

What did you do with that information?
I started learning how big of a problem it was. At the time, less than 0.1 percent of US venture capital dollars were being invested abroad. I had conversations with the UK and the Spanish consulate and got positive feedback. International started to seem like an interesting thesis. The companies are undervalued, so if you can find those great companies, investors will want to meet them. I thought you could showcase them in a big pitch night, and voilà – success. But I realized it was too big of a problem. Pitch nights weren't the answer.

What was the answer?
US investors were not willing to invest in foreign startups. We needed to find a pathway to the US market for them. The answer was building a platform to support these companies and enable them to sell and raise capital in the US.

How do you do that?
I worked to understand the checklist for investors and learn what kind of traction companies had to have in the US to be considered investable. Then I helped build a program so that companies could check off all the things on that list. On the list: You have to be a Delaware C-Corp; own the intellectual property your company is based on; have a founding-level senior member in a US office; and most likely be attacking the US as a primary market of focus. You need a minimum level of traction, and you need to prove that whatever product-market fit you found at home works here.

And then we took that list and started helping companies on their way to US success.

What are the accelerator programs like?
We have a one-week "hyper accelerator" program and three-month "US launch" program. The focus is to hyper-grow your network and imprint the best practices that leading companies use across sales, marketing and fundraising. We work with teams to set up the footprint that will lead to sales traction with US clients and help them tell the story that raises capital.

The one-week programs are like conferences, except that instead of being one in a thousand people at a conference, they're one of ten or twelve around a boardroom table. They get this cohort experience with other CEOs running companies just like theirs. Then we blast open their networks with more than twenty-five thought leaders who'd otherwise be hard to get in front of. They get to hear them speak and shake their hands, so they can put that relationship to work. They do all this without having to sacrifice ninety days of distraction from their businesses.

“For the last five years, I’ve had 6 to 10 meetings per day, on average taking 30 to 50 meetings a week, 120 to 200 meetings a month. It’s my superpower.”

Foreign founders are higher-risk entrepreneurs; they don't know how this marketplace works, they don't have a network, and they're already doing something impossibly hard: building an exit-able tech company. We're helping to offset that risk and accelerate them through the process, in just four days.

How many programs do you run?
Today, we're doing this at scale. That means twenty-five to thirty one-week programs and four or five cohorts of the three-month programs every year

How do you manage all the relationships needed for the accelerators, like with mentors, investors and speakers?
For the last five years, I've had 6 to 10 meetings per day, on average taking 30 to 50 meetings a week, 120 to 200 meetings a month. It's my superpower, and it allowed us to grow really fast initially. The team has taken on that mentality too. When we were smaller, we leveraged a small network of contacts doing a lot for us. We had to communicate and add value to the people coming to speak. If you're bringing good companies to investors, they're getting opportunities. They were typically unwilling to hear pitches from international companies, so we had to do a lot of education about why ours were different. For investors, it's all about the quality of the companies, so from the beginning I was really obstinate about finding the best companies.

We ended up building a brand within the tech ecosystem where investors and experts can be confident that we filter highly and that the companies will be relevant. And, for mentors, it's a great opportunity. Fintech investors get to meet ten awesome fintech companies. Media businesses get to meet fifteen entrepreneurs in the new media space who are creating augmented reality platforms or battling against information warfare and fake news. The density, focus and quality of our programs is what adds value. Quality is the real lynch pin. The quality of companies is what really brings people back and keeps them involved. And that's true of any accelerator, innovation program or venture fund... it's all about the startups.

Why did you extend your program to US companies?
What happened was that we started running some sector programs. FinTech was first, since it was a natural fit with my network and with New York. We were recruiting a cohort of the best FinTech startups around the world, and it would be disingenuous to not have any from San Francisco and New York. Now, it's about eighty percent international and twenty percent US.

How did you figure out your business model?
We run the programs in one of two ways. Either we build it and run it, and companies pay a fee for coming; or we have a sponsor – like a foreign government or corporation with a cohort of companies they want us to support from seed to growth – and then we build it and run it on their behalf.

Figuring out a revenue model wasn't easy. I advise dozens of business in and out of our programs. To anyone who's trying to build a business that provides services to startups, we say not to focus on companies with no budget, which often fail at a rate of 95 percent. But that's the market we're building a program in, so I'm not taking my own advice. But it's about building a brand and a community, defining the most efficient process for US expansion and then raising a fund to support companies through that process. That's why I don't take my own advice.

What was hard about building VentureOut?
It was revenue funded. Early on, I worried about things like being able to pay rent. I solved that by doing consulting work on the side for the first two years, and this challenge put me in the seat that hundreds of our founders have been in. The experience made me unbelievably empathetic to the people we're serving. VentureOut is for entrepreneurs by entrepreneurs.

What was the best decision you made along the way?
Two years ago, we decided to start running sector-focused programs. This taught us that relevance and focus was everything. Instead of running general programs for a mixed cohort of companies, suddenly every founder, every investor, every corporate exec – everyone – was aligned. We also accelerated our own learning, becoming deeply informed in fintech, artificial intelligence, retail and e-commerce, enterprise software, virtual reality and blockchain; we now have our finger on the pulse and are intimately aware of the needs of companies innovating in those sectors. It was a small decision that transformed our business.

[About] VentureOut **helps post-seed companies navigate the New York technology ecosystem through short-term accelerator programs. For international companies, VentureOut offers a foothold into the United States, while sector-specific accelerators connect groups of founders to relevant investors and clients.**

[Links] Web: **ventureoutny.com** Facebook: **VentureOutNY** Twitter: **@VentureOutNY**

What are your top work essentials?
MacBook Pro, iPhone X, Flux Charger, Karma hotspot, Yeti coffee cup and a presentation clicker.

At what age did you found your company?
Twenty-nine.

What's your most-used app?
FoodKick: same-day delivery of beer and food for events and the office.

What's the most valuable piece of advice you've been given?
Be unbelievably passionate about whatever it is you're trying to do.

What's your greatest skill?
I'm a networker. My superpower is being able to take more meetings than any other person in NYC.

Clayton Banks

Cofounder / Silicon Harlem

When Clayton Banks, a cable and communications professional, realized that technology would drive businesses and communities into the future, he decided that the only way to make sure that the coming shift would benefit all players equally was through infrastructure. His idea was to broaden broadband access and share expertise with communities like Upper Manhattan who weren't by default at the forefront of the technological shift. In 2014, he incorporated Silicon Harlem, a for-profit social venture that works with networks to provide state-of-the-art broadband and runs the annual Next Gen Tech Conference, an event that attracts tech leaders to the neighborhood and brings together entrepreneurs and businesses to turn Harlem into a buzzing tech hub.

Why build a tech hub in Harlem?
Twenty-first-century life and the economic engine behind it are rooted in technology and innovation, so in order to ensure that urban markets and dense areas like Harlem don't get left behind, it's important to build the infrastructure that allows for startup activity, such as incubators, coworking spaces, accelerators, and capital funding. I'm looking for those types of communities to thrive.

What's the importance of physical spaces, like coworking spaces, to technology innovation?
We've found that the most important driving force for the future is inclusion. How do we get more voices to the table? When you look at technology and innovation centers, a large part has been centered on the West Coast where there's not as much diversity as in New York City. Having physical places in your area allows you to populate it with people from a variety of perspectives and backgrounds. That's New York's advantage. In order to build the economic engine of the future, you need technology companies here, now.

What does diversity bring to tech?
One of the incredible realities of this moment is that we're moving into the fourth industrial revolution, and it's being defined largely by technology and innovation. Everyone and everything will be connected. When you look at the infrastructure, you see it'll require all voices, whether rich or poor; it'll require all voices to ensure that the next infrastructure we build for our country creates equity in access and exposure. It's not the easiest way to get things done, but it's valuable. That's why one of our values is to make sure we're inclusive in everything we do.

How did you decide to start Silicon Harlem?
One thing I identified early on was how, as we moved from analog to digital, incumbents in the telecom industry were struggling. You needed a wave of capital to go from a typical operating center to a digital platform, and it was so difficult to make that transition. I decided to explore software and next-gen connectivity. That took me from traditional cable to the advanced technology business, which includes both optical networking and wired and wireless connectivity.

That was a driving force: to be part of the future. Having worked in traditional communications, I knew I had a lot to say and to share with people who haven't had that experience. At the same time, living in Harlem and having that exposure also motivated me to want to ensure that people who are often left behind, who are marginalized or trailing, had access to the information I had access to. I thought if they got it, we could make a difference in how things function.

How did you build the community around Silicon Harlem?
I saw a window where advanced communications could be deployed in upper Manhattan. We could galvanize the community and get them focused and thinking around technology and innovation.

After that, we addressed the educational aspect of all this, thinking about how much people in the area know about broadband, the Internet of Things, etc., and how all of that relates to the infrastructure being upgraded. The idea was to start with exposure, and have that drive adoption of new technologies and interest in them. In our area, 40 percent of households didn't have high-speed internet at home, not only because of lack of access but also lack of exposure and high cost. First, I wanted people to get the connection. Now, we have to work to get the price down so it's affordable.

How did you go about educating and exposing the community to tech?
We've been emphasizing how important it is to incorporate and substantiate science, technology, engineering, and math learning in the public school system. We've worked with the Department of Education to deploy after-school programs. That's how we've been able to touch the lives of young people in our city with concepts they can take on with them to college. The Caribbean Culture Center has retained us over the last four years for STEM camp each summer. We have hackathons, and events for senior citizens to demystify tech, and last year we taught people to build their own video games. The point is, we touch lives.

"People always have the same goal: to improve the quality of life. If we all get that, then every year we should try to find new tools in our toolbox to make that happen."

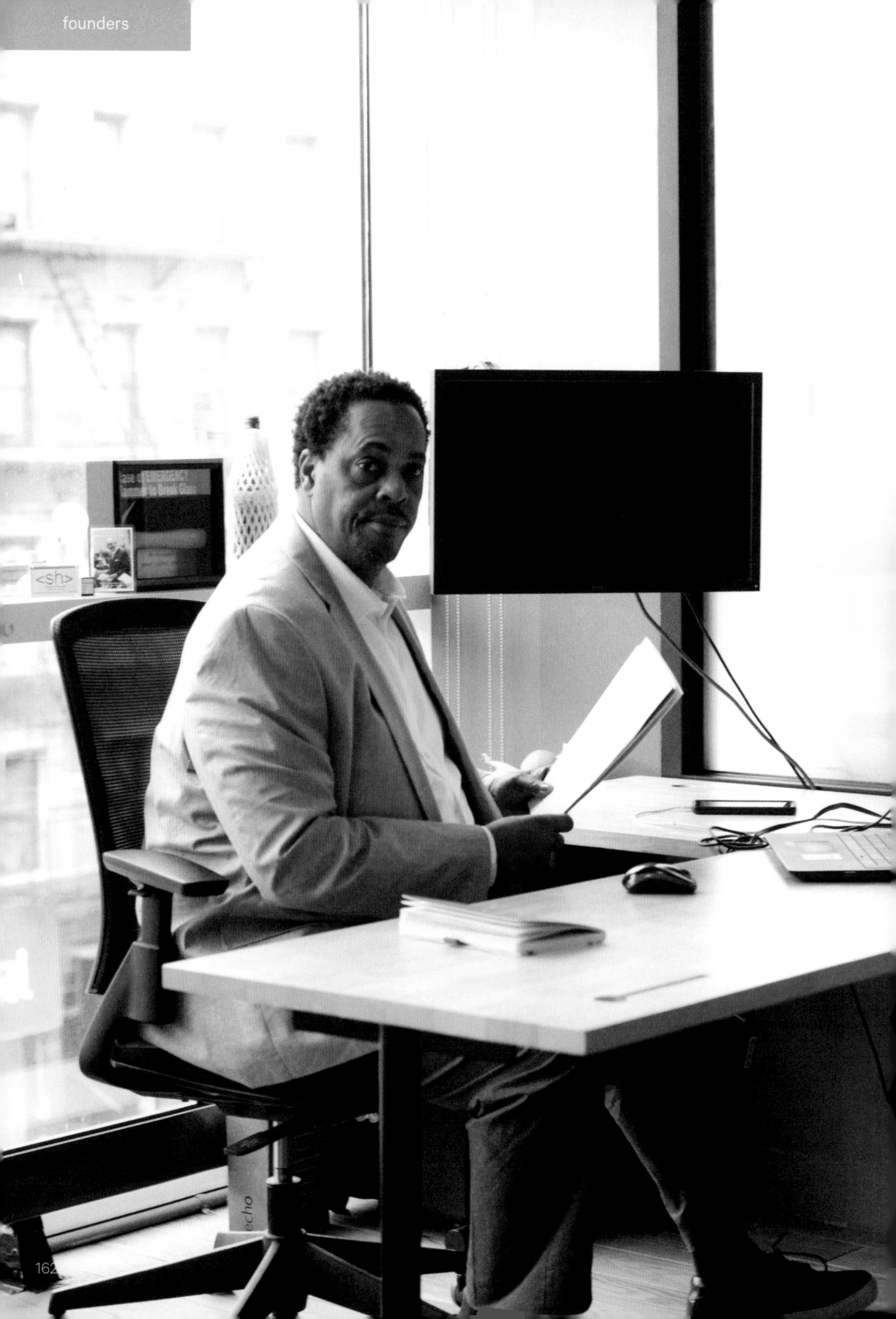

What are the best decisions you've made as you built Silicon Harlem?

We've created our entire business philosophy to be citizen-centric. We weren't as focused on what we could do from the technology perspective or digital literacy or education. We were most focused on asking, What are the current issues the everyday citizen is facing in our community? We wanted to find out what the deal is here. And we found out about issues outside of tech, like noise, garbage and vermin. When we can talk about those things, not just how fancy our router is, we make the connection more deep and intimate. Then, when we share tech-enabled solutions, there's an acceptance level. That's something we're proud of. Even when we created our first meetups, which featured experts, they were really designed to bring the community together. We had reputations for writing white papers and going to Congress and talking to politicians and academics and high-level private sector folks, but once we realized a bottom-up strategy was working, it made our trajectory clearer.

We also wanted to focus on building an ecosystem based on communication: being able to communicate with our elective officials, the academic community. Columbia and City College are right here, so it made sense for us to speak that language, and we wanted to make sure it resonated in the private sector too.

What was the moment you realized your idea was working?

We held a big meetup. We were always going downtown for tech meetups, so we said, let's do one uptown. Five hundred people came out to our very first one. We were like, "Maybe there is something up here." From that point on, we were doing meetups every month or so, and big crowds kept coming out.

Also, the first conference – our Next Gen Conference. We had good attendance and experts from all over. It was eye opening to see our vision come to fruition. When we saw the people tied into the idea of the hub and serving people new tech and innovation, that was an aha! moment.

What mistakes did you make?

One of the things we're still a little challenged by is how we manage resources. To build a tech hub, attract companies, get people connected to the internet and do digital literacy means lots of resources. We have to be more aggressive in raising capital. There are so many opportunities coming our way, but without the resources to accommodate, we have to move more slowly.

Did you raise money from outside firms?
We're completely self-funded. We're making an offering for the first time this year. It took the first four years to build our brand and to build loyalty. Now that this platform is built, we feel it's time to build resources and accelerate. We're looking at private institutions rather than crowdsourcing. We'd rather have a large partner involved who can continue to capitalize us as we grow.

What advice would you give other entrepreneurs?
Be clear with what you're doing: don't try to do everything. Get a customer.

What would you tell other community builders in the tech space?
Galvanize the community first. Think of our name: Silicon Harlem. It creates a perception shift, connecting Harlem to Silicon Valley. For us, part of the challenge is making sure that the perception is there. Creating a great brand is important. You have to solidify the anchors that not only build the hub but also sustain it – focus on people and not on tech. People always have the same goal: to improve the quality of life. If we all get that, then every year we should try to find new tools in our toolbox to make that happen. That's what tech has done rapidly: create the tools to enable life to be better. And that's the ultimate outcome for anyone innovating, building tech hubs or building companies. It all leads back to the person. You're humanizing technology.

What do you like most about working in New York City?
I love the people. I love it in all different ways. There's nothing better than going from neighborhood to neighborhood, and I just love the architecture of New York. We're suited to be one of the greatest cities in the world because of topology, and the diversity and the comradery. There's no more loyal person than a New Yorker.

[About] Silicon Harlem **is a for-profit social venture intent on building a tech ecosystem in Upper Manhattan. Led by Clayton Banks, the organization accomplishes this by building community through events and at coworking spaces, advocating for the adoption of high-speed connectivity and encouraging tech innovation and investment in Harlem.**

[Links] Web: **siliconharlem.net** Facebook: **siliconharlem** Twitter: **@SiliconHarlem**

What are your top work essentials?
Computer, mobile device, great design and visuals.

At what age did you found your company?
Fifty, but I've been thinking about it since I was nineteen.

What's your most-used app?
Google Drive.

What's the most valuable piece of advice you've been given?
Keep an eye on the bottom line.

What's your greatest skill?
Negotiating and communication. I love talking.

Harry Kargman

CEO and Founder / Kargo

Harry Kargman is the CEO and Founder of Kargo, which develops mobile advertising campaigns and technology for major companies across multiple industries. Harry attended Harvard University, where he studied government and computer science. After graduating, he built his company without any outside investment.

Tell me a little bit about yourself and how you got to be where you are today.
I've always focused on the intersection of tech and its practical applications for the day-to-day, and through that I fell in love with the mobile phone. I believed that the mobile phone could effectively become the remote control to people's lives: a screen you could use to access the world around you and a device where you could store all of your information and stay in touch with friends. For a number of years, Kargo built sites and apps for publishers, as content needed special optimization to be accessible on the mobile screen. As publishers learned to do that on their own, what they really needed was monetization through advanced ad technology. Kargo became one of the largest players helping tier-one brands and digital-only content brands pivot and build an audience on mobile devices.

What was it about the mobile phone that really captivated you at that time?
Getting out of school, I was focused on the television screen. I worked for a company called Intertainer that developed consumer content experiences for TV. It allowed you to go through a list of every movie or television show you'd ever want, buy or subscribe to it, and stream it live to your television screen. But what we realized at the time was that we couldn't deliver that experience cost-effectively without participation from the cable networks and access to broadband. Given these insurmountable limitations, I saw the mobile browser as a bigger opportunity. As I fast-forwarded ahead, I imagined faster networks and bigger screens. It was obvious to me that mobile would dominate how and where we get information. When I came to that realization in 1999, I jumped in and started Kargo 1.0. But it was too early, and that company failed. The technology didn't mature as fast as I'd hoped, and I came to learn the lesson that it is not only vision but the timing of the vision that dictates success.

I restarted Kargo in 2003, having lost my prior team and funding. Even then, I thought it was only a matter of two to four years before the mobile screen would dominate media channels. I didn't think that it would take until 2013 for it to mature to where it is today. Looking back, I definitely didn't appreciate how timing can extend out. I timed it wrong twice, but I had the determination, persistence and sureness of my insight and vision to believe that mobile would eventually become a major vertical and channel in people's lives.

What does today's version of Kargo look like?
Kargo creates mobile brand advertising, marketing technology and ad formats for brands to get consumers to pay attention and take action on the small screen. Whether it's familiarizing consumers with a brand or even getting them to buy a product, Kargo sets the standard for what mobile advertising should look like. It's hard to serve and target nearly 200 million people a month, and we want it to be easy for our customers to work with us to ensure that this happens. Pretty much everybody in the United States has seen one of our advertisements – probably once a month or even every week. Our format's look and feel is non-intrusive and respects the consumer experience, and it's meant to look beautiful and interesting.

Could you give me a successful example of that?
I can give you a couple of good examples. This year, we created a store locator functionality for Reckitt Benckiser. That functionality displays how easy it is to find their products, where those products sit around your location, and why their product is better than other similar products on the market. In the past, we ran a campaign with Unilever around their Magnum ice cream bars, which tended to sell out really quickly in locations during the summer. They needed to deliver that message based upon weather — the hotter the better — and help their customers find their products easily. Later this year, we have new products coming out I'm even more excited about. We've been struggling with the fact that consumers don't watch more than six to ten seconds of video ads on their phone. Most marketers are trying to take their thirty-second television spots and repurpose them for the mobile screen, hoping the consumer will watch for thirty seconds. That isn't happening. For the first time, we've worked with one of our large brands to pioneer the development of a six-second and ten-second spot. We've never done this before, but it's never been done by anyone. We just went out and shot our first series and delivered the first edits this week, and we're really excited to experiment more with the format and structure.

"Whatever your big idea is, it almost never ends up being the thing that makes you super successful."

HARLEY DAVIDSON
KARGO

What's your advice to an early-stage founder who wants to get started in the entrepreneurial field?

My general advice is that whatever your big idea, it almost never ends up being the thing that makes you super successful. You're always pivoting to something else, and it's always a work in progress. It took me more than four evolutions to get Kargo right. So, if you think you have a big idea, that idea probably won't work as you envisioned it in your business plan. Simply being in business and being an entrepreneur will get you there, especially if you listen closely to the market and are not risk-averse to putting your prior business model out of business. The second piece of advice is to build in enough of a cushion of time, staying power, and your own personal drive to get through those low points. Do you have the wherewithal and resolve to weather the setbacks? The third thing is that you need to understand yourself. Almost nothing that really makes money, makes money on the first day, month, or year. You need to find success in what you do, not in how much you make. If this is your get-rich-quick scheme, it almost never works out. The final piece of advice is be conservative about your expectations. Try to do as much as you can by yourself in the early stages. To the degree that you can, have a small team and work out what works and what doesn't. Don't make big bets. Make small bets and watch them through. This way, when it comes time to raise money or continue to organically build a company from revenue, you have a careful view on the business and can ensure that you can survive if the business environment turns against you.

We talked earlier about timing. Is there anything you would have done differently with Kargo?

Things always take longer than anybody anticipates, especially in a new technology area. You can disrupt an existing business that's already well-established pretty easily if you have a slightly new take on it. The idea of picking a new area where there's a lot of opportunity means you'll have to wait it out. I think I could have achieved more success earlier had I picked a smaller team, worked in an existing area where there was already a larger proven market opportunity, and found a disruptive model. In this case, it's more about execution than it is about the big idea. The biggest opportunity if you're a lifelong entrepreneur is to figure out a new area that you're passionate about, where you can make a contribution, and where you're willing to pivot a few times before actually getting it right. In this regard, you have to have supreme self-confidence as you come up with an idea that most people will not understand or get behind until it has proven out.

Looking back on your fifteen-plus years of experience, do you think there was a single best decision that you made?

I don't know that there was any one best decision that I made. I think it was multiple decisions in concert with an ever-changing market that got us to where we are today. The market and the ripeness of your opportunity are like a twisty river. As long as you continually point your bow directly upriver, and have a strong engine, you can make progress. However, in moving forward, if somehow your business model starts to misalign with the market and you don't pivot and adjust fast enough, your bow shifts off center and the current starts pushing you into a rotation. You're still motoring forward but your energy starts pushing you in the wrong direction, and you rotate away from the opportunity. Eventually you get turned around, go backwards, and are dead in the water. The question really is, Where are you today, what is the market asking for, and can you keep the bow of the ship directly pointed toward the opportunities in the market? I think it's that core focus that's so pivotal in determining success and failure.

What is the best thing about working in New York City?

What I love about New York is the inspiration all around you. I believe that the best creative minds in the world are in New York: art, fashion, media, finance and design. In terms of finding people who are passionate about the things that you're passionate about, there's no better source of human capital. Also, just the sheer number people who come to New York City to find opportunity, even if they start somewhere else, is amazing. I think it's a great city because of the diversity of different businesses that operate in New York. So, if you want to be in a place where many of your customers and partners are already based, there's frankly no better place in North America. It's really this core concentration of people in your industry as well as creatives, and this collective inspiration, that makes it such an amazing place to start and grow a company.

[About] Kargo **is a leader in the mobile advertising space, having worked with clients across the publishing and advertising industries, including everything from Vice to Johnson & Johnson. Kargo works with advertisers and publishers to develop creative, artful and fun mobile ads.**

[Links] Web: **kargo.com** Facebook: **kargo** Twitter: **@kargo** Instagram: **kargomobile**

What are your top work essentials?
Phone, travel earphones, MacBook Air, small pocket notebook and charger, Jack Spade briefcase.

At what age did you found your company?
Twenty-five.

What's your most used app?
LinkedIn, but Zoom for communications.

What's the most important advice you've been given?
"If you stir shit, it smells worse."

What's your greatest skill?
Convincing people that a non-obvious idea is the right direction to go in.

Kevin Ryan

Cofounder and Chairman / AlleyCorp

Kevin Ryan is a founding force of the New York City tech scene. In 1996, he joined then-tiny ad startup DoubleClick and became its president and CEO. In 2005, after DoubleClick's sale, he and Dwight Merriman, one of DoubleClick's cofounders, formed AlleyCorp, a startup holding company. They looked for opportunities to capitalize on the transformation the Internet was bringing to so many business sectors. They began to start several companies per year, including ShopWiki, a shopping search engine; Gilt Groupe, the flash sales site; Business Insider, a digital media property; and MongoDB, a database company that went public in 2017.

Why did you get into technology by working at DoubleClick?

I was thinking of launching a company in the ad sales or ad tech space, because I wanted to understand the landscape. I'd been working at the media company E. W. Scripps, which owned the rights to Dilbert and Peanuts. In 1995, I launched a Dilbert site that became successful. We were selling advertising in some of the first online ad deals and doing e-commerce. I concluded in 1996 that the Internet would be the most fundamental thing I'd see in my lifetime. I thought I'd start an Internet company on my own, but then I met the founders of DoubleClick, which was six months old. They said, "Come join us." I thought they'd created an amazing piece of technology, so I said yes.

How did the idea for AlleyCorp come about?

Dwight and I were working together after leaving DoubleClick. We had an idea for a company, and then we realized we had another idea for another company. We thought, What do we do? We figured we could diversify our risk a little. There's a risk that you work on a startup idea for four years and then it's not adoptable. But if I started a few companies, the odds of one working were high. I could scale myself. Normally, you're either a founder or CEO, or you're an investor who invests in others. I wanted to do a hybrid where I was a serial founder who could later move to chairman.

What do you do day-to-day as a serial founder?
I consider myself an operator. I'm not an investor – though I put in seed money. My day-to-day is working with CEOs to help them manage the companies. I have more experience because I'm so old. For example, I've done thirty-five rounds of financing. No individual CEO would have that experience.

How have good business relationships allowed you to build so many companies?
I have a lot of repeat relationships. For example, the Zola team, Shan-Lyn Ma and Nobu Nakaguchi, both worked for me at Gilt. When we had the idea of e-commerce in the wedding space, I thought they were perfect. Now their entire senior team is from Gilt.

Another example is CoEdition, a clothing company. Their cofounders all worked with me at Gilt. And the three founders of MongoDB. We all worked at DoubleClick together. Gilt and DoubleClick are two of the few companies that actually have reunions every year. Three hundred and seventy-five people who worked at Gilt at one point showed up for a Gilt reunion party. I host and pay for the party to maintain those relationships.

And what have you learned about building teams?
I don't think I have some great way of figuring out who a good person for each job is, but I think people are open and willing to come work with me or for me because they call around and ask if I'll be supportive. People have to take a real leap of faith and maybe a pay cut, and they have to work hard. I spend a lot of time keeping in touch and looking for talent all the time. I spend most of my time on people.

What do you like about starting companies?
I love the challenge. You have an idea, and you go into a new space. Most startups don't work; you have to compete against much bigger companies or figure out why no one has done this idea before. That's a big business challenge. Once you do that, you can't go back.

At a legacy company, if your goal is to grow revenue by one percent over last year... I can't get excited about that. In a startup, everything matters. Every new sale is a record. There's a focus, excitement, challenge. It's arguably the hardest thing to do in business. The mere logistics are challenging in real time: building systems, commission structures, accounting systems.

It also just so happens that this twenty-year period has been the most exciting startup period in the history of the US and the world. Entire industries have changed. In seven years, Business Insider has three times the traffic of The Wall Street Journal and has displaced it in terms of being the number-one publication that people read. Thirty years from now, I think Insider will still be number one.

"You have to make decisions before something is obvious. If it's obvious, your competitor probably made that decision five months ago, and it's too late."

mongoDB

There was a magic period because the Internet was the one huge technology shift of the century, and there was an opportunity. Take wedding registries. People have been using wedding registries for fifty years. In three years, Zola disrupted that. Another company I'm involved with is a mobile bank in Argentina. We signed up two thousand people in a few months. Two years after starting, we'll have five percent of all bank accounts in Argentina. No bank has grown that fast in two years, because in the old way you had to open branches, and you can't do that quickly. I'm in all of these industries where you can start up with relatively little capital. People forget that twenty years ago, there were almost no startups.

What early struggles did you have to overcome?
When you do startups, so many things go wrong. The biggest one was in 2000. At DoubleClick, we had two thousand employees and I was feeling pretty good. Three years later, we had a thousand employees and the stock price was down to $5 a share. That doesn't make you friends: not with employees nor with investors. We did seven rounds of layoffs, and I had to turn over the entire management team. DoubleClick was a provider to other websites, and seventy percent of our clients went bankrupt. We had huge losses and write-offs. There were people I knew well, whom I'd convinced to quit their job and come work for us, that we had to fire nine months later. That is tough.

We got out of it. We reduced our costs. You have to think of it as if you had gangrene on your arm. The right thing, at some point, is to cut off your arm; but those are tough battlefield decisions. Eighty percent of our competitors went bankrupt. We increased our market share during those three years and came out much stronger compared to others. We got through and became powerful again, worth $1 billion in 2005.

What were some of the best decisions you made along the way?
One that was good and risky was choosing Henry Blodgett as cofounder for Business Insider. Most people in journalism will tell you that you can't have an editor-in-chief who hasn't been a journalist, because he won't have credibility. If you choose someone who's been banned from Wall Street and you're doing a business publication, people will say that's insane. For the most part, the people I interviewed were exactly who you'd expect: senior editors at business publications. I thought Henry would be a better choice, though I knew it would be either a terrible idea or unconventional and brilliant. In the end, the success of Insider is due to him. He's been brilliant and innovative.

Did you make any mistakes along the way?

Often, everything you did in the previous year is a mistake. At DoubleClick, I bought a Scandinavian ad network for $100 million, and two years later it was worth almost $0. Before the 2000 crash, I signed a ten- or fifteen-year lease for two thousand people. I think I paid $50 million to get out of that lease. They weren't terrible ideas when we did them, but they turned out to be mistakes. Along the way, there are people you hire and realize you made a poor decision, and you fire them six months later.

You have to think of it like a professional athlete, though. At first, you'd think that if a hitter gets a hit one out of every three times, that's terrible; but then you find out he's the leading hitter in the major league. People will strike out two out of three times.

Knowing that strikeout rate, how do you make decisions?

You have to make decisions before something is obvious. If it's obvious, your competitor probably made that decision five months ago, and it's too late.

At DoubleClick, we expanded internationally before finding out whether our model worked in the US. We went to twenty-five countries, we lost money and made mistakes. But large companies did business with us, because I could service them anywhere in the world. Then we became the big player. Yet, once in a while, you realize I just made the same mistake in twenty-five countries.

What advice would you give people in the early stages?

Remember that you're learning. You're finding out who your customer is. Also, whatever you're doing at the startup, your job matters. Startups are successful if they hire great people.

What is great about working in tech in New York?

The tech industry here isn't so full of itself, because unlike San Francisco we're just one of many industries here. In a one-industry town, it ends up being too much, and a level of arrogance creeps in. With so many industries here, we know we're not that important. If you're running an art museum or a Wall Street firm, then you're the top, but not if you're working in tech. Also, we're number two to San Francisco, which makes us more humble and more collaborative. Everyone in tech knows each other and has worked together. We all want New York tech to succeed. It's just a small industry. I think people really like working here.

[About] AlleyCorp **is a holding company for startups in industries including software, e-commerce, healthcare and media. By launching new companies and building out their founding teams, AlleyCorp has found a way to scale entrepreneurship and apply the expertise of its cofounder, Kevin Ryan, to more than one growing company at a time.**

[Links] Web: **alleycorp.com**

What are your top work essentials?
My phone and iPad. Reading material, since I'm a big newshound.

At what age did you found your company?
I started in startups at age thirty-two.

What's your most used app?
Email and Business Insider.

What's the most valuable piece of advice you've been given?
Tom Murphy at DoubleClick said, "I want you to do the right thing." I knew exactly what I needed to do.

What's your greatest skill?
Working with people.

Liz Wessel

CEO and Cofounder / WayUp

A graduate of the University of Pennsylvania with majors in political science, math and Japanese, Liz Wessel founded her company WayUp at the age of twenty-four. Despite her age (she's now twenty-seven), she's something of a serial entrepreneur with three startups already under her belt. Liz met her WayUp cofounder JJ Fliegelman at UPenn, and eventually the two left their full-time jobs to develop their startup, doing so through the Y Combinator incubator. They originally called the company Campus Job but ultimately settled on the name WayUp, which, Liz says, she much prefers. In 2016, Forbes Magazine named Liz one of their "30 Under 30 In Enterprise Technology." She has also appeared on lists of the top one hundred entrepreneurs in "Silicon Alley" as well as Silicon Valley. At WayUp, she now heads a team of sixty-five employees and manages a user base of 4.5 million people.

Tell me about yourself. What's your background and how did you get into the entrepreneurial field?
I was born and raised in New York City, then moved to Philadelphia to go to UPenn, which is where I met my cofounder JJ Fliegelman. At Penn, JJ and I really bonded over our mutual frustrations with the process by which college students look for jobs and get recruited by employers. After graduation, I ended up working at Google – first in Mountain View, and then in India – and at Google, I saw from the other side how hard it is to recruit college students and recent grads, because there's so much quantity and it's hard to find great quality.

Between those two experiences, and from having developed a love of entrepreneurship from various small businesses I started throughout college, JJ and I both decided to quit our jobs and start our company together. That's the high level, but essentially we started out of a frustration that we ourselves saw first-hand.

Let's talk about WayUp. You saw a need and decided to do something about it. What was the first step you took toward actually creating a company?

When JJ and I were in college, we worked on a side project related to WayUp that helped college students find a part-time job. Later on, when JJ and I both agreed to quit our jobs and start a company together, it was really a matter of learning as much as we could about the domain, about the space, and about the problem, as well as how other companies had tried to solve the problem. From there, it was just about getting educated on the issue and ramping up as much as possible.

Did you always consider yourself to be an entrepreneurial person growing up? Like, were you the type of person who ran lemonade stands growing up?

Definitely. The first time I sold things was to sell Barbie Dolls at the local park. I'd get Barbie Dolls for Hanukkah, and if I got bored with them about a week or so later, I would go sell them. Then, in elementary school, my dad would give me $2 bills, and I would go sell the $2 bills for $3, $4 or $5. I got in trouble with the school principal, but I just thought it was a smart business move. In high school, I started various organizations and extra-curricular activities. Then, in college, I started several companies, one of which I ended up franchising throughout the country. I've always loved creating something from nothing.

What have been some of the greatest challenges in putting WayUp together?

There's no shortage of challenges. I'd say, first and foremost, the biggest challenge is figuring out what you need before you need it. That's everything from having a team that can scale with you to making the right product decisions, and so on and so forth. I also think just planning and focusing your time can be really hard. You need to figure out what is the highest leverage way you can spend your time, and it's often a lot harder than it sounds.

Was it scary to leave your full-time position to dive into a startup? What was it like for you to make that transition.

Not really. I always wanted to start my own business and work on it full time, and even my boss and team knew that for the entire two years I was at Google. In fact, I told the Google recruiter this before I accepted my offer!

“No matter what age you are, you’re always going to have imposter syndrome.”

If you could start WayUp again from the ground up, is there anything you'd do differently?
We started the company under a different name, The Campus Job, and it was a terrible name. About a year later, we changed it, but I wish I'd just started with the name WayUp from the start.

What differentiates WayUp from Idealist or Indeed or other job sites out there?
At WayUp, we're focused as much as possible on quality. We don't want you to apply to as many jobs as possible, and we don't want employers to have to sift through thousands of candidates in order to hire just a few. Our goal is really just to help find the right match. What that means, first and foremost, is that we help employers make sure that their jobs are being shown to the right candidates through machine learning, filtering and lots of other tools. We also help both sides of our marketplace – our employers and our candidates – look really attractive to the other. As a result, early-career professionals and companies can make sure that they're telling their stories to the right people.

Could you talk about the growth of the company since it was founded?
It's been about four years, and we're now at about sixty-five employees. We have about 4.5 million users. We've just been growing really quickly in many aspects.

In this process, would you say there's one single best decision you've made in terms of steering the company forward? Have there been any particularly difficult decisions you've had to make?
The most important decision has definitely been related to building the team. We've hired so many incredible people, though of course we've also made mistakes with hiring, too.

How does it feel for you to be relatively young and be a CEO of a quickly-growing company? Do you ever feel overwhelmed by that?
I don't feel overwhelmed because of my age. I was speaking with some other CEOs yesterday about the fact that, no matter what age you are, you're always going to have imposter syndrome. I don't think that's because of my age; I think it's because this is a new role for me. I've never been a CEO before, and more specifically I've never been a CEO of WayUp before. In fact, no one has been the CEO of WayUp before. So there's this feeling of, "I don't know if this is the best business decision for me, for the company, and so forth." But you just have to surround yourself with smart people and hope that you're making great decisions while

knowing sometimes that you'll make a mistake. My age hasn't been a really big factor except in the very positive sense of being able to know that I'm not too many years different from the average user on WayUp. I remember very clearly what they're going through and what that experience was for me, as well.

What can we look for going forward with WayUp?
You can expect us to continue to help as many people as possible. We're completely obsessed with focusing on helping our users find a role that they'll enjoy. We like to say our tagline is "Meet your future." We want to help as many people as possible meet their future and meet a better future – both in this country and hopefully one day in the world.

What's your favorite thing about working in New York City?
I can safely say the tech scene in NYC is incredible. While it's not as big as the tech scene in San Francisco, it's growing really quickly. Everyone is so supportive of one another here. No matter what sector you're in, how much you've raised, what you look like, or how old you are, everyone is so helpful to one another. We're all committed to making New York the next great tech hub. In Silicon Valley when I was raising my Series A, I had a couple of investors say, "Are you really moving back to New York? How are you going to be able to grow this business? No great tech companies have been grown out of New York." I'm happy to say that they've been proven wrong many, many times.

[About] **WayUp, founded in 2014, is revolutionizing the job-search process for recent college graduates and employers. The platform, a two-way marketplace, helps college graduates find jobs and internships, and helps employers find the perfect applicants for their open positions, while also providing tips and advice for both parties.**

[Links] Web: **wayup.com** Facebook: **wayupinc** Twitter: **@wayup** Instagram: **wayup**

What are your top work essentials?
My phone, my computer, my team, my notebook, and a cold brew.

At what age did you found your company?
Twenty-four.

What's your most used app?
Captio.

What's the most valuable piece of advice you've been given?
Make sure you find a career that you love, because you'll probably spend more time with your career than with your spouse.

What's your greatest skill?
My work ethic.

Mina Salib

Founder of Usspire / Program Manager, Future Labs at NYU Tandon

Mina Salib's career in technology is driven by a relentless curiosity. As a young professional, he sought to understand how technology innovators had gotten their start and launched his own company, Usspire, to document the stories he collected. The project pushed him into the technology community. As he attended tech events and meetups, he befriended the city's tech founders, investors and other stakeholders. Eventually, the networking landed him a job organizing a pitch competition for New York University's Tandon School of Engineering, which propelled him to his current position as program manager for Future Labs, a network of business incubators created in partnership with New York City.

What did you do before working in technology?
I actually started out as a pre-dental student. Then, in my last year of college, I decided to forgo dental school and try to get into business. I was never formally taught business. Starting out, real estate was the only thing I could get into without any business credentials, so I got my license and did a few deals.

How did you get into tech?
By starting Usspire, a media company with a goal of inspiring and providing solutions for ambitious millennials. Usspire was about me wanting to learn from other founders how and why they got started with their companies: the real stories people didn't always talk about, not just the good times. I didn't have a formal community or know anything about tech. I started going to meetup events, like Startup Grind, which is run by two of my now-close friends.
For Usspire, I would interview as many founders as I could meet, typically people under the age of twenty-five, since that's how old I was too. I wanted to learn how young, diverse, millennial founders got their companies started.

What were the big takeaways from all your interviews?

Many people didn't have a lot of family support – not that their families didn't want them to be in startups, but in a financial way. This was a big risk for people. They started from nothing and had a hope or a vision. They wanted to see the world in a certain way and build companies towards that mission or goal. That taught me that purpose is important. You need to have a goal bigger than yourself when starting a company. Learning that these founders who didn't have all this support were taking this risk meant that their cause was worth it to them, and that's different from the companies that get covered in traditional technology media. Other than that, I learned some cliché things about building a company, such as having determination, being efficient with dollars, and having good team dynamics.

What happened with Usspire?

I ended up with two employees and a couple of interns and grew readership to ten thousand readers. I built it up through social media. A lot was the network effect: people like to have their story told. I thought if the people I covered were sharing the stories with their networks, others would hear about the publisher Usspire. That led to newsletter signups and followers.
Then, I was offered a role at Tandon.

How did you decide to move on from your company?

That was a hard decision. Especially when you're first starting out, every entrepreneur thinks their company will be the next big thing. I learned that in media, it's hard to create consistent cash flow; when you don't have millions of viewers, it's hard to make ad revenue. It's still a success, though, even if the company is not generating substantial capital, because it leads to your next career move. You weigh the pros and cons, and be honest. You can keep burning cash or you can make the move that the company set you up for.

What would you say are the most important skills a founder should have when starting a company?

In my opinion, self-awareness is the most important quality a founder can possess. It gives founders unique insight into their strengths and weaknesses, which allows them to build a team that complements and optimizes their skills. Those who are self-aware also tend to understand how their actions, words and initiatives affect others. This is an essential practice, because founders should consistently gage team morale and know when it's time to adjust tactics in order to keep their team happy, inspired and productive.

“The city motivates you. It is a motivator of its own. There is greatness everywhere, and you want to be a part of that.”

WINERY

What is something about the entrepreneurship journey that you wish you'd known at the start?

I wish I knew that success comes at a different time and in a different form for everyone. Many times, it's not the first experience but rather the compilation of multiple experiences that leads you to that "big thing" which allows you to make the impact you seek.

How else are you involved in the ecosystem?

I've done a few angel deals. I've been lucky enough to get in on some syndications of deals as well. I did that because it gives me more of a stake in the success of a company. It's easy to consult and then walk away, and not have skin in the game. When you take the next step, actually invest, you then live or die with them.

What were your early struggles in New York's startup world?

I have so many, so I'll limit it to one. The biggest mistake I ever made was comparing myself to anybody else. I think early-stage founders, especially founders without a lot of work experience, compare themselves to peers, to people they see on any of the numerous tech outlets, or to their friends on social media. You're around a lot of founders, and everyone has a different trajectory. I've seen some startups have a month of success and then flame out. I used to compare myself to that: why don't I raise more money, have that great partnership, get that media coverage? It makes you go for a lot of things that don't last – quick hits. That hinders your growth, because that time you spent comparing yourself and reaching for something you don't deserve yet because you haven't put in the work could have been used building an actual foundation.

The second biggest thing is, plan but don't plan. Have goals and a vision for your life, career and business, but realize it's okay if things change.

What about the best decisions?

Those are very few. The really great one was starting my company. It taught me what tech is and how to build a business. It laid the foundation. And the next was finding very close people I wanted to work with in my career. Being at Future Labs for as long as I've been here, I realize that there's always a lot to be done. The last two years, I've sucked everything out of every opportunity, and I've found people I want to work with long term.

Would you start another company?
Yes. For now, the next big thing we're focused on is the city's first AI accelerator, AI NexusLab. The question is really, how can I help build out NYC AI? The goal for that is to try to make New York City the commercial AI hub of the world by bringing the best startups from around the world and merging them with the best corporations in the world. My role is being a conduit between those startups and the companies looking for their technologies. We're in the process of building out those partnerships now.

What professional advice would you give people in the early stages of starting up?
Doing your research to begin with: know the market you're getting into, and see if what you're trying to give to the market is needed. As much as there are books like Lean Startup and lots of blogs and Medium posts full of tech news and advice, a lot of founders don't actually test their ideas, because they're scared of what the market will say.

I don't think founders do enough of that – creating innovative ideas and then testing them in the market. I'll get on the phone or meet someone for coffee and suggest some research, and then find out they haven't even done the Google search on their topic.

Don't be worried about the fact that you're not the first person to think of your idea.
That doesn't mean you shouldn't enter the market, even if there are other competitors, because execution is key. Execution really wins out – not how much venture backing you have. Pick your early team wisely: know who you're going into business with. The best teams have the best founder dynamics. Often, places will vet people but not notice how they work with others. Know what culture you are building early on, and understand the people you're building it with.

What do you like about working in New York City?
The city motivates you. It's a motivator of its own. Even if you take away the people – obviously the people are on their grind – there is greatness everywhere, and you want to be a part of that.

[About] NYU Tandon Future Labs **offers a variety of programs to help scale early-stage companies. Program Manager Mina Salib acts as a bridge between the startups in Tandon's many accelerators (which cater to certain types of founders or sectors) and the investors, advisors, resources and infrastructure those new companies need to contribute to the NYC economy.**

[Links] Web: **futurelabs.nyc** Facebook: **TheFutureLabs** Twitter: **@NYUFuturelabs**

Mina Salib / Usspire / Future Labs at NYU Tandon

What are your top work essentials?
My laptop, AirPod, glasses, phone and coffee. Then I can work from anywhere.

At what age did you found your company?
Twenty-three.

What's your most-used app?
Spotify.

What's the most valuable piece of advice you've been given?
The right thing is always the right thing.

What's your greatest skill?
Making people feel comfortable.

Ragy Thomas

Founder and CEO / Sprinklr

Ragy Thomas was leading an email marketing company around the time that social media platforms were taking off. As he watched the community-building and brand-building on Twitter, Facebook, and LinkedIn, he saw an opportunity: no companies were offering a comprehensive social cloud software product that could bring together all their social media needs, from marketing to customer service. So, he started one. Since 2009, Sprinklr has grown into a 1,400-person company with twenty-two offices around the world and clients across Fortune 500 companies and government agencies.

What did you do before starting Sprinklr?

I was president of Epsilon Interactive, which was part of Alliance Data Systems (ADS). We'd sold a previous email startup to them in 2005, and I was one of the principals who built out Epsilon. My background and previous startups were in email marketing. I've been fortunate to have the opportunity to see how consumers moved from phone and letters to email as a primary way of communicating with each other. In my previous business in email marketing, we'd built platforms for enterprises to use email as a communications channel for customers and prospects. When I saw Twitter, YouTube, etc., taking off in 2006 to 2008, it was clear to me that businesses would have to start using social media channels in a more foundational way than they were. I'd seen this movie once before.

How did Sprinklr solve social media for companies?

The idea was to invent the unified platform to engage with and listen to customers across all channels. I had the insight that this was a great opportunity because of the fact that social media solved fundamental problems for companies the same way we had with email. Email is one dimensional. For example, it doesn't support permissions, so someone can spam you. And it doesn't support photos and videos as well as social media, which can do livestream and private inboxes really well. These were all problems I'd seen in commercial marketing;

and Twitter, Facebook, and LinkedIn all solve these problems: if you don't want to hear from me on LinkedIn, you just unfriend me; they all support multimedia; and they all have different messaging capabilities. We thought they would take off and that there would be an ability to do what we'd done in email, and we saw that from the beginning. That was a differentiator we had from day one.

What is the range of Sprinklr's products?

We have six primary offerings, which you can also buy as one unified platform. The Social Cloud includes social publishing and social engagement, and there's also social listening in that bundle, which helps companies see and understand what people say about them, with a whole slew of capabilities to do this at scale. There's the Content Cloud for influencers. With the Advertising Cloud, you can advertise, report, and optimize – you can run your advertising campaign on all social media platforms through Sprinklr. The Research Cloud collects insight, branding, and location information through advanced AI and analytics. There's the Commerce Cloud, which gives you ratings, reviews and shoppable galleries. Last, you have your Care Cloud, which is an end-to-end customer cloud solution.

How did you think to add customer service to social media management software?

Out of the gate, we were trying to be a complete social media platform, a place you could publish to twenty-six channels, listen and advertise across all the channels. To be able to do that, we had to come up with constructs that unified the front office.

Think of a large enterprise brand. There are many different business units, and each of those operates in multiple countries. And for each product in each country, they market and advertise and need customer care. To market in each country, they might use five to six channels. Yet, internally, the teams managing these channels can be siloed or not even talk to each other. Because of the nature of social, business use cases from advertising to customer service all mix. I might be a marketing manager at a company like Nike or Microsoft and post a product update on Twitter. But right underneath that, someone could post a customer service issue, like, "Oh, your return policy is horrible." Now the poor marketing manager is saying, "What do I do with this?"

Early on, we had to build queuing, routing and other intelligent ways of connecting people across operational silos so that this kind of thing wasn't a problem.

“I like to tell people that Sprinklr is unapologetically the most ambitious company and group of people you’ve ever met.”

How did that change your vision?

We realized, a few years in, that we were the first software that enables companies to let teams work across internal silos. That led to our aha! moment. We're the first purpose-built software that connects across channels and silos, with a unified set of data for customer, content and campaigns binding it all together. The unified platform for front office was a big idea – bigger than social media management. I like to tell people that Sprinklr is unapologetically the most ambitious company and group of people you've ever met. We think we're sitting on a massive opportunity, and we're just getting started.

What did previous leadership roles teach you about founding a company?

You always learn new stuff and make new mistakes. Sprinklr has been a very different journey than Epsilon. With scale comes intensity. As a leader, you have to evolve from when a company is in its founding stage to when it's in its growth stage to when it's in mature stage. Sprinklr is in a growth stage. I had to transform to become that operational CEO and founder.

What was a notable mistake along the way?

One of the lessons I learned the hard way was to recruit for culture. There was a year we hired four hundred and fifty people, and, as you scale like that, you think, I just need people to fill the seats. Then you look back and realize you didn't take the time to ensure a culture match. The culture of the company is what you have to protect through thick and thin. That was a painful learning experience.

How did you create a successful hiring philosophy?

The key is to be very precise with who you're looking for. A lot of the time, recruiting becomes about who's available, especially in companies' early stages. What I've learned with Sprinklr is to be a lot more intentional with who you're looking for, down to what you want them to look like, sound like, feel like, and think like. Developing the mental model with relentless detail allows you to spot the person when you find him or her.

What early struggles did you have?

Going back to scarcity mode. I went from running twenty-three offices at Epsilon Interactive to working in my spare bedroom to start Sprinklr. That was harsh, going from that kind of executive life back to the pure startup grind. But, it was also really fun. In my previous run, when we were a small company, we dreamed of making it larger. But after selling to a public company,

I realized that the best part of the journey is the early days, when you're struggling. In the second go-round, you learn to appreciate that a lot more than you did before.

Also, being discounted by others' shortsightedness. In our early years, because our vision was larger than our competitors, the market didn't understand what we were up to for the longest time. While some of our point-solution competitors got acquired, we appeared to be left behind. That was a struggle from a marketing and sales perspective. There were a few years before the need in the marketplace became a perfect match with our product.

How did you overcome the left-behind feeling?
We didn't have to overcome it. That's the beautiful thing about being far-sighted. It's just a matter of time until the world catches up to what you believe in, if you saw it right. Think of Amazon and how relentless they were with vision and strategy. We kept getting dressed down for not making money through our expansion and our customer-first craziness. You just ride it out. The scale and success – which come because you believe in the strategy, and it was right – that's what gets you out of it.

What was the best decision you made?
We acquired eleven companies, and the best decision was to keep rewriting everything into a unified codebase after an acquisition. Every time, we'd throw away the code and rewrite it into our platform, because it's important to preserve a unified codebase when you're building a platform. If the codebase isn't architected well, it will break down and not be elegant and scalable. Those were some of the worst short-term pains we took on, but in hindsight that's one of the best decisions.

What do you like about working in New York City?
I just love the energy. New York is a special place where you have a lot of different industries. It's very balanced. It's not all technology. And you have such a heterogeneous environment. Diversity in their environment makes all organisms strong. New York is like that.

[About] Sprinklr **is a social media management software company that aims to provide companies with a full front-office solution by enabling teams to collaborate across internal silos and to succeed in realms ranging from marketing to customer service.**

[Links] Web: **sprinklr.com** Facebook: **sprinklr** Twitter: **@sprinklr**

What are your top work essentials?
My cell phone. I am never away from it, to a fault.

At what age did you found your company?
Thirty-six.

What's your most used app?
Skype. I'm constantly connected to the rest of my team.

What's the most valuable piece of advice you've been given?
Effort doesn't matter, results do.

What's your greatest skill?
Finding patterns across large, diverse bodies of observational data and behavior.

Shan-Lyn Ma

CEO and Founder / Zola

Shan-Lyn Ma is the cofounder and CEO of Zola, an all-in-one online wedding registry and planning company. Shan-Lyn was born in Singapore and grew up in Australia before moving to the United States to attend the Stanford Graduate School of Business in 2004. Before founding Zola, she worked at Yahoo!, Gilt Groupe, and Chloe and Isabel, Inc., focusing on product development and management. She has lived in New York since 2008.

Tell me a little bit about yourself. How did you end up doing entrepreneurial work?
I was born in Singapore and grew up in Australia. My dream had always been to work in Silicon Valley because that's where a lot of the companies at that time were emerging. I didn't know anyone who had ever worked in technology or who had ever worked in the US, but I'd read that a lot of the great tech startups were started out of Stanford University. I thought that must be the way that you have to go, and so I worked really hard to get myself to Stanford. I did my MBA at the Business School, and then got to work at my dream company at that time, which was Yahoo!. That gave me my first taste of what it was like to be in the thick of it in Silicon Valley. I fell in love with products: product management, product development, thinking about product alongside great technologists and designers. I moved to the US in 2004 and have never looked back.

Did you always know you wanted to be an entrepreneur?
I always really wanted to start something myself for a couple of reasons. One was that I didn't grow up with a lot of money, so I knew that if I wanted to do things, I had to go and earn them myself. No one was going to do them for me. I was also a bit nerdy as a child. I'd read business magazines, and I'd always admire entrepreneurs who had paved their own path and created something out of nothing. I found the idea of that to be magical.

Where did the idea for Zola come from?

The idea for Zola was born, like many startups, out of personal need. The year we started, 2013, was the year that all of my friends were getting married at the same time, and I was buying a lot of presents from their wedding registries. Because my background is in e-commerce, I found the e-commerce shopping experience of buying from the registries to be the absolute worst. I started to talk to my now-cofounder Nobu about it, because he and I had worked closely at Gilt Groupe designing products, and we'd always talked about starting something together. We both felt we could do a much better job, creating a much easier, more beautiful wedding registry that our friends would really love and want to use.

What are some of the differentiators between Zola and some of the other e-commerce wedding registry sites out there?

Before we launched Zola, the wedding registry market was dominated by the big traditional department stores. What we found in interviewing hundreds of engaged people was that couples today have very different needs from couples in the past. They really want physical gifts, experiences and/or cash all in one wedding registry. The second big realization was that couples today get married at an older age and invest a lot in their wedding day. They want their wedding registry and every component of their wedding to reflect who they are as a couple. Zola is still the only registry that couples can fully personalize and customize. Our platform is available on any device, and what we hear again and again from our users is that Zola is just easier than anything else out there.

What was the toughest or the best decision that you made along this path?

One of the toughest decisions was figuring out the right time to launch additional products beyond registry. For the first three years in business, we focused 100 percent of our time and energy on building the best possible registry for our couples. Once we'd fully cleared product-market fit, we started to think about the next product we should launch beyond the registry. We had a lot of couples asking us for different things, but ultimately we realized that the most popular request was for Zola to help couples in designing their wedding website. So, last year we launched our second product, Zola Weddings, which includes free wedding websites, a guest list manager, and a custom checklist of all of the to-dos to help you plan your wedding. It was a big decision because it was the first time we were expanding beyond our initial product, but it ended up being the best decision ever because it has grown phenomenally.

"As an immigrant, growing up with very few resources given to me, I realized that I had to work harder than anyone else."

Looking back, is there anything you'd have done differently?

The philosophy at Zola, and something that Nobu and I wanted to have as a key part of our culture, is to be very fiscally responsible. We want to make sure that we're not burning capital unnecessarily. As part of that, we've been very thoughtful about each person we've added to the Zola team. But, in the beginning, we were almost too thoughtful, and there were some roles we could have benefited from hiring earlier on. Now we think about how to bring people on in a thoughtful and fiscally responsible way, but we don't wait until it's an absolute fire drill before we really need someone in a given function.

What advice do you have for a young entrepreneur in New York who's trying to found a company?

Before you commit your most valuable resource, which is your own time, be really sure that the idea and the business model is absolutely the thing that you want to commit to 24/7 for at least a decade of your life. Sometimes the life of an entrepreneur is glamorized, and it's not until you're in it that you realize it really requires a lot of grit and grinding it out. In order to get through the journey, make sure that you've done all the work upfront to confirm that you have the right business idea and the right partners in place, so that you can then feel comfortable committing your time and a big chunk of your life to something that's going to be all-consuming.

A lot of the greatest entrepreneurs come from an immigrant background. How has the experience of being an immigrant shaped you?

I think it definitely made me more determined and focused on getting to the place I wanted to go as quickly as possible, because I knew I was here for a reason. I wanted to build something with a lasting impact on the world in the same way that other tech companies have. In order to do that, I needed to be focused and driven. As an immigrant, growing up with very few resources given to me, I realized that I had to work harder than anyone else.

What have been some of the challenges for you as a woman in a very male-dominated field? And have you seen any changes in that inequality over the past five to ten years?
I've started to see more female founders start companies, but traditionally it has been extremely challenging for female founders to raise VC funding, because most VC investors are men. If a female founder is solving problems she experiences in the market, it's often harder to pitch a product to male investors who are not the targeted end user. With Zola, I certainly found that I'd get questions from certain investors who didn't really understand the need or the pain point and who found it hard to relate to the business and the product. Ultimately, those are not our investors, and we're lucky to have great investors, both men and women, who deeply understood our customer, the pain points we're solving, and the market. There's also a movement starting in the VC industry to have more female investors, and I think that will have the biggest impact on the funding, support and infrastructure for female founders.

What's your favorite thing about this city? What's the one thing that makes New York New York for you?
I moved to New York from the Bay Area about ten years ago, and the thing I loved when I first moved to New York is still my favorite thing about the city, which is the hustle of all the people who live here. I think no matter what their job, no matter where they live or what their socioeconomic status, everyone here is a hustler. They're driven, motivated and they want to make it work. That is something I love and get inspired and energized by. From the people I work alongside on the Zola team through to the people performing on the subway and trying to earn a dollar, everyone here is always learning, iterating, seeing what works, and then trying to make it better for themselves and for the people around them, and I just love that.

[About] Zola **is a one-stop shop for couples planning their wedding, with a store of over sixty thousand gifts from over six hundred different brands. Couples can register for a free wedding website builder, a guest-list management tool, and other resources. Zola allows couples to streamline and customize their big day.**

[Links] Web: **zola.com** Facebook: **zola** Twitter: **@Zola** Instagram: **zola**

What are your top work essentials?
My notebook and pen, lipstick, laptop, my phone and my coffee.

At what age did you found your company?
Thirty-five.

What's your most used app, other than Zola?
Let's see. The weather app.

What's the most valuable piece of advice you've been given?
Always think about how something can be bigger and more ambitious.

What's your greatest skill?
Never giving up.

sch

ools

- **Get good grades and score high on entrance examinations.** Columbia admits only the best and brightest students from across the country and around the world.

- **Demonstrate leadership.** Columbia looks for well-rounded individuals who have demonstrated leadership in their own academic careers prior to applying to university.

- **Be bold.** Having some experience in the startup community is a really good marker that you're not fearful of pursuing a course that may not have a well-prescribed path in front of it.

- **Show outside-of-the-box thinking.** Just getting really good grades in high school and great SAT scores is not enough to get into Columbia. Combining best practices around academic achievement with the notions of risk-taking, innovation and creativity that you generally associate with entrepreneurs can make your application stand out.

[Name]

Columbia University

[Elevator Pitch]

"Each of our seventeen schools and institutions has a particular focus on innovation and entrepreneurship. Our students and alumni can plug into the startup community with classes, programs and funding opportunities – all within America's second-biggest locus of new venture creation, New York City."

[Enrollment]

More than five thousand students and alumni are engaged in Columbia entrepreneurship programs or pedagogy.

[Description]

When it comes to entrepreneurship at Columbia, there is no one-size-fits-all approach. "Pick your focus, customer problem and solution, and then add an entrepreneurial approach to the application," says Chris McGarry, senior director for entrepreneurship in the University Office of Alumni and Development. "We have seventeen different schools and institutions, most of which have some focus on a practical or commercial application for innovations, which means innovators across Columbia are translating theory and applying it to the real world to make their vision a reality."

Columbia offers a depth and breadth of opportunities that are perhaps unmatched in the entrepreneurship space in New York City. Students can not only take courses in entrepreneurship but also participate in the Columbia Venture Competition, innovate at the Columbia Design Studio, or investigate blockchain at the Columbia Blockchain Studio. Across the various schools – from the Business School and Columbia Engineering to the Graduate School of Journalism – students and alumni can find concentrations in entrepreneurship and programs aimed at sparking innovation, such as the Tamer Center for Social Enterprise at Columbia Business School, and the Brown Institute for Media Innovation at the Journalism School. Recent alumni can join the Columbia Venture Community, a separate 501(c)(3) organization that matches recent grads with networking opportunities, or apply to work at Columbia Startup Lab, a 5,100 square-foot coworking space in SoHo. Columbia also gives $2.4 million in funding to founders each year through grants and competitions.

"The president of Columbia is committed, both philosophically and practically, to the innovation and entrepreneurship programming offered across the University," McGarry says. And with good reason. Entrepreneurship not only benefits Columbia students but also attracts the next generation of talented students. "The people who are accepted at Columbia University are also likely accepted at one of our peer institutions," he says. "Our strong entrepreneurship programs help Columbia attract the best students and best entrepreneurial talent that the world has to offer."

[Apply to]

columbia.edu

[Links]

Web: **entrepreneurship.columbia.edu** Facebook: **columbiaEship** Instagram: **columbiaEship**

- **Be engaged.**
  We're looking for students who are really "switched-on." That's a hard thing to quantify, but basically it means that you're curious, competent and eager to collaborate with others to better the world.

- **Go the extra mile.**
  Admissions at Cooper Union uses a multifactor approach to analyze who gets admitted into the college. For engineering applicants, the following criteria are evaluated: high school grades and course selection, SAT/ACT scores, SAT Subject Tests, essays and letters of recommendations. Architecture and art applicants must also submit other unique requirements, such as portfolios and home tests in order to be considered for admission.

- **Be a leader.**
  Not only do students need to develop high levels of technical knowledge in their discipline, they also need to know how to recognize and act on opportunities to make change.

- **Collaborate.**
  Communicate well with others and build something amazing.

[Name]

Cooper Union

[Elevator Pitch]

"We're a rigorous school with a culture of creativity and making that feeds off and feeds into New York City's rich entrepreneurial environment. Even though we don't have an entrepreneurship degree, we were rated the top entrepreneurial college in Forbes Magazine."

[Enrollment]

853 undergraduate; 74 graduate

[Description]

Invention is in Cooper Union's blood. Founded by inventor Peter Cooper, who designed the first American-built steam locomotive, the Cooper Union for the Advancement of Science and Art is one of the best places for aspiring inventors and innovators – not only in New York City but across the US. With leading undergraduate-level and graduate-level degree programs in architecture and engineering, as well as an undergraduate program in fine arts, Cooper Union prepares students for creative pursuits by engaging them in a hands-on learning experiences. It's been called one of the nation's "best design schools for creative talent," one of the top ten "colleges that pay you back," and it ranks among *The New York Times*' "most selective colleges."

"The secret of Cooper and its successes have a lot to do with our mission – to inspire inventive, creative, and influential voices in our core disciplines of engineering, art and architecture," says Eric Lima, associate professor of mechanical engineering. "Our amazing location at the intersection of 7th Street and 3rd Avenue also contributes. There's no separation between 'campus' and city. When Cooper students walk out of class, they're in the heart of the city; they have to figure it all out. So by the time they graduate, they have competency that goes well beyond academics."

Cooper Union engineering students are constantly being challenged to create, whether that's through classes like Engineering and Entrepreneurship, or Principles of Design, or through programs like the Invention Factory that give students the opportunity to develop and test a product over the course of a six-week intensive accelerator summer program. "Cooper is a gem," says Eric. "It is a small school, so the students create Cooper Union anew every year."

[Apply to] **cooper.edu/admissions**

[Links] Web: **cooper.edu/welcome** Facebook: **cooperunion** Twitter: **@cooperunion**

- **We look for students with a strong academic background.**
  We're particularly interested in technology-related fields.

- **We look for students with an entrepreneurial or independent spirit.**
  Independent entrepreneurs take the initiative and don't wait to be asked or told.

- **We want students who want to work in an interdisciplinary environment.**
  Working with other people who are studying the same thing you are is the norm in academia. Working on a team with people from different academic backgrounds is more challenging, but you often get better outcomes.

- **We want students who want to build something.**
  You must be able to apply what you learn in a practical way to create something useful to people.

- **We want students who have the desire to use digital technology to help meet human needs.**
  This is core to Cornell Tech's beliefs.

[Name]

Cornell Tech

[Elevator Pitch]

"We're bringing together a set of disciplines that are important for digital-age product development and doing it as a collaboration between academia and industry."

[Enrollment]

300 students in the past academic year.

[Description]

Cornell Tech aims to create pioneering leaders and technologies for the digital age through research, technology commercialization and graduate-level education. Cornell Tech offers Masters programs in computer science, information science, electrical engineering and operations research as well as an MBA and law degree, and doctoral and postdoctoral study programs. "We're building a very special environment," says Dean Dan Huttenlocher. "It's a mixture of first-rate academics with top practitioners performing real-world product development."

Cornell Tech was born in 2010 when the City of New York issued a challenge to top institutions from around the world to propose a new or expanded applied sciences and engineering campus in New York City. In 2011, then-mayor Michael Bloomberg selected a joint proposal from Technion – Israel Technology University and Cornell University from a pool of eighteen applications. In 2017, after spending five years in Google's New York City building, thirty faculty and three hundred students moved into the first phase of Cornell Tech's permanent campus on Roosevelt Island. The campus currently houses the Tata Innovation Center, where students and startups work side-by-side on new ideas; the Emma and Georgina Bloomberg Center, which serves as Cornell Tech's learning hub; and a residential building. When completed, the campus will include two million square feet of state-of-the-art buildings and over two acres of open space, and it will be home to more than two thousand graduate students and hundreds of faculty and staff.

Cornell Tech's curriculum is unique in that all students, regardless of major, spend a substantial portion of their curriculum in Studio, where they form interdisciplinary teams to create working prototypes of product. "We're creating a mock of what the real work environment is like, to help students learn how to put their expertise into practice," says Dan. "It's product development in an academic context." Tuition at Cornell Tech is $54,584 for a Master's degree, $65,456 for a law degree and $102,652 for an MBA.

[Apply to] **tech.cornell.edu/admissions**

[Links] Web: **tech.cornell.edu** Facebook: **CornellTech** Twitter: **@cornell_tech** Instagram: **cornell_tech**

- **Get good grades.**
  We are quite selective, with fewer than half of applicants accepted to the university and an average incoming GPA of 3.64.

- **Follow through.**
  We like to see students that demonstrate a commitment to something. Rather than seeing a student who has ten activities, we'd rather see somebody who has two or three that they were very involved in.

- **Be a leader.**
  Maybe you started out as a member of the coin club, then you were on the executive board, and then you developed a blog around coin collecting. Whatever it is you're interested in, we look for students who are very involved and who demonstrate a commitment to that involvement.

- **Demonstrate curiosity.**
  Fordham students are looking to solve the world's greatest problems. Asking questions is a key part of this.

[Name]

Fordham University

[Elevator Pitch]

"We offer an applied, practical approach to all our disciplines. Whether you want to be an entrepreneur, you already are one, or you're still in a period of discernment, there are a variety of ways to become engaged."

[Enrollment]

15,582 students, of whom an estimated 15 percent take entrepreneurship courses.

[Description]

If you want to understand why Fordham University sits at the forefront of New York City's entrepreneurship ecosystem, look no further than the university's Jesuit roots. The school's founder, John Hughes, was an entrepreneur, being the first person to bring Catholic education to the city. So too was the founder of the Jesuits, Ignatius Loyola, who laid the foundation for the largest network of higher education institutions globally. "Innovation and applied learning were always part of a Jesuit education," Donna Rapaccioli, dean of the Gabelli School of Business, says. "Maybe the story wasn't being told."

Perhaps it should be. With more than fifteen thousand students across nine schools, many of whom study entrepreneurship to some degree, Fordham is among the leaders in the entrepreneurship space. The university runs its own small business incubator called the Fordham Foundry, offers courses across its two main campuses in everything from "Executing the Entrepreneurial Vision" to "Small Business Finance," and facilitates a network of changemakers through the Social Innovation Collaboratory, to name just a few of its activities. Each year, students are invited to pitch their business and social enterprise ideas with the possibility of winning $20,000 in prize money at the Fordham Foundry Pitch Challenge. In addition, a small cohort of freshmen participate each year in a yearlong fellowship with the Kenneth Cole Foundation aimed at creating socially conscious businesses that solve the world's greatest problems.

With campuses in the Bronx and Manhattan, and partnerships with Fordham's law and business schools as well as many corporate partners, Fordham offers a truly diverse experience for students across the spectrum of entrepreneurship. "One of the advantages of Fordham is that we have a truly collaborative environment, and the students across all the schools really do work together," Donna says. "There are so many opportunities for the students to tap into what's happening in the city, and they do."

[Apply to] **fordham.edu/apply**

[Links] Web: **fordham.edu** Facebook: **FordhamUniversity** Twitter: **@FordhamNYC** Instagram: **fordhamuniversity**

- **Be multifaceted.**
  Ultimately, the thing that makes a student most likely to be successful here is what you might call institutional fit. We're looking for the kind of learner who demonstrates an engagement with both creativity and innovation, as well as with complex sociological and urbanistic issues.

- **Demonstrate engagement with the world.**
  Both in the work you do prior to coming to undergrad or as a graduate student in your undergraduate studies, you've really taken stock of where you see yourself engaging the world.

- **Be self-directed. We're looking for engaged innovators.**
  That's a particular kind of student: the kind who will do well in the self-directed and entrepreneurial environment.

- **Excel in your subject area.**
  Be able to combine specific subject area knowledge with a willingness to collaborate.

[Name]

The New School

[Elevator Pitch]

"We're the number one and largest independent art and design school in North America. We offer a wonderful mixture of a comprehensive full-service art and design school within a university."

[Enrollment]

10,000 at The New School, 5,500 at Parsons School of Design

[Description]

In an era where young people are increasingly being asked to excel at not just one thing but many, finding a school that gives students the freedom to truly work across disciplines is paramount. And at the New School, hybridity – the idea of breaking down borders and finding solutions that work for everyone equally – is the name of the game. Located in the heart of Manhattan, the New School is a design school, undergraduate liberal arts college, and graduate school all in one. With ten thousand students and a number of offerings in the entrepreneurship field, including academic courses, programs and funding opportunities for startups, it's also a great place for students to ideate, innovate and collaborate. "Innovation and startup culture are infused in almost all of our programs," says Joel Towers, executive dean of Parsons School of Design at the New School. "There's a built-in culture of innovation because of the types of programs we offer."

These offerings include a minor in entrepreneurship at the School of Design Strategies; a graduate program called Impact Entrepreneurship Venture Lab, which focuses on socially conscious innovation; Elab, an on-site design incubator that also offers year-long fellowships for designers and entrepreneurs; and entrepreneurship courses at the undergraduate and graduate level. More broadly, both the New School as a whole and Parsons School of Design specifically seek to integrate design and innovation into all angles of the student experience, which is aided, of course, by being in a city where design seeps into every industry, from journalism to fashion. "Students who want to make change in the world do so in an environment that's increasingly complex," Joel says. "Amidst all of the hybrid, crossover, cross-disciplinary, and intersectional approaches, there's also a deep commitment to excellence and specific subject area knowledge."

[Apply to] **newschool.edu/apply**

[Links] Web: **newschool.edu** Facebook: **thenewschool** Twitter: **@TheNewSchool** Instagram: **TheNewSchool**

inve

stors

- **Be the right founder.**
  At least one of the company's cofounders must be a woman. This is non-negotiable.

- **Differentiate your innovation.**
  A venture investor is really looking for those ones and zeroes – some sort of differentiator, usually a technology differentiator – that separates you from the pack.

- **Network, network, network.**
  The best thing always is to find someone who knows us well and who can make an introduction. We've met with people who made a cold approach, but we'll always take a meeting if the intro comes from someone we know and respect.

- **Know your market.**
  We look for founders building for a consumer they know, someone whose needs and desires they understand. It helps if they have brand in their DNA and know what a good brand looks like.

- **Combine conviction and adaptability.**
  Be able to think three steps ahead, but also be willing to accept feedback.

[Name]

BBG Ventures

[Elevator Pitch]

"We back founders transforming daily life: expanding access, creating materially better products and services, or simply bringing delight to the mundane. As the dominant consumer, women are uniquely positioned to do this, so all of our investments have at least one female founder."

[Sector]

Commerce, media, marketplaces

[Description]

Despite making up half of the US population, women represent just 5 percent of startup founders and 7 percent of partners at top venture capital firms. Does that mean women simply aren't cut out to be entrepreneurs? Certainly not. The reasons for these discrepancies are numerous, but, despite incremental progress being made to level the playing field, one factor continues to hold women back: a lack of access to capital. In fact, in 2017 female-founded companies received less than 3 percent of venture capital investments.

As CEO of Gilt.com, a fashion and lifestyle website, Susan Lyne saw this firsthand. "I met a lot of young women who were starting companies, and they all had a similar experience raising money," says Susan, now president and founding partner of BBG Ventures, a VC firm that invests in female-founded companies. "The partners around the table were all men, so before they could pitch their business, they had to explain how women think about X, or how women make purchase decisions."

Lyne started BBG Ventures to bridge the gap and, in the process, invest in some of the premiere companies reshaping industries from media to consumer goods and technology. Since September 2014, BBG has made fifty-five investments across two funds, which, according to partner Nisha Dua, makes it the largest portfolio of female founders in the country. "We think that having a woman on the founding team is a unique competitive advantage," Nisha says. BBG has invested in everything from GlamSquad (on-demand beauty services) to goTenna (communication devices that work when there's no service) to The Wing (a coworking space and social club for women), with the typical seed investment ranging from $300,000 to $500,000. "New York City is a great place for female founders," Lyne says. "It's a much more heterogeneous business environment than Silicon Valley, the VC ecosystem is younger and more fluid, and there's a growing community of women who want to see you succeed."

[Apply to] **hello@bbgventures.com**

[Links] Web: **bbgventures.com** Twitter: **@BBGventures** Instagram: **builtbygirls**

- **Show me why you're the right person to start the company.**
  I look for things I can eliminate: things like the market is too small or the skill-set of the founder doesn't meet the challenge of the company.

- **Set the right goals.**
  I want to make sure that our plans set the company up in a way that can be most successful. A founder shouldn't come in and pitch for an $800,000 round if she needs $1.6 million.

- **Do your research.**
  Make sure you do a thorough job talking to everyone in your field. I'm looking for founders who are not going to be taken by surprise.

- **Be original.**
  Too often I meet with a founder, and there's already some New York company that's tried something similar and things didn't work out. Did you reach out to them? Did you talk to them? That should be your first due diligence as a founder.

[Name]

Brooklyn Bridge Ventures

[Elevator Pitch]

"I run the first venture capital firm to be located in Brooklyn. I'll invest in any New York company, regardless of industry, that has yet to raise $750,000 in a previous round."

[Sector]

Multiple

[Description]

Manhattan might boast the city's tallest skyscrapers, the fanciest restaurants, and the most halal carts per capita, but Brooklyn has something that Manhattan doesn't: the people. With a population of almost one million more inhabitants than Manhattan and a total space that far exceeds that of "the city," Brooklyn's comparative advantage is its size. That's a big part of why Charlie O'Donnell, sole partner and founder at Brooklyn Bridge Ventures, based his VC firm in the "Borough of Homes and Churches." "I live in Brooklyn, and, like a lot of entrepreneurs, that's where I have my community," Charlie says. "I'd venture to say that over fifty percent of the tech community lives in Brooklyn."

Since 2012, Brooklyn Bridge Ventures has invested $23 million in over sixty companies across two funds. Charlie will invest in any company that's yet to raise $750,000, which, he says, tends to be the "the toughest check to get." He was the largest seed investor in The Wing, a coworking space for women; he led the seed round for Canary, a home-security company; and he invested in Industrial Organic, which operates an organic waste processing facility.

Charlie hears about two thousand ideas each year but has time to meet with only about 7 or 8 percent of the people who pitch him. He's constantly filtering to get down to the best, most well-researched and realistic of those ideas, he says. But that doesn't mean that he's not open to everyone he meets. Charlie hosts dinners across the city – from Bed-Stuy to the West Village – and sends out a weekly newsletter to more than thirteen thousand subscribers. "I strive to be as accessible as possible," he says. "I don't think the best deals going forward are all straight, white bald guys. If I get an opportunity to back people with diverse perspectives, I'm going to do that."

[Apply to] **Charlie@brooklynbridge.vc**

[Links] Web: **brooklynbridge.vc** Blog: **thisisgoingtobebig.com** Twitter: **@ceonyc** Instagram: **ceonyc**

- **Be a good communicator.**
  We're looking for passionate founders who can also communicate their ideas well. If you can't explain it to us, how can you explain it to your customers?

- **Be able to recruit and retain a team.**
  Likewise, we're looking for founders who can get others to agree to come work with them.

- **Get coffee with us.**
  We don't do applications. Introduce yourself, come hang out, and use our network, your references and your relationships to find us.

- **Collaborate.**
  We help each other out. If you're not working on something, you help one another out and learn together. It definitely encourages a lot more collaboration, and of course creative pursuits come out of that.

[Name] # Expa

[Elevator Pitch] *"We're a global network of entrepreneurs helping each other to build companies. We partner with founders to create new products and services, and build teams to scale them as independent businesses."*

[Sector] **Software**

[Description] Expa isn't a typical investor, nor is it a startup accelerator or program. Rather, the company inhabits the grey area between the two. Founded in 2014, Expa is a startup studio that places a premium on collaboration. If you've got a great idea for a company or you're looking to work with other entrepreneurs on an idea that may not be your own, Expa is going to be there building it alongside you. "We don't sit around listening to pitches," says Naveen Selvadurai, partner at Expa. "We help build a team and a product, and also fund that early team from within and help get it to product-market fit."

Led by a powerhouse of entrepreneurs, including Naveen, who cofounded Foursquare; Garrett Camp, cofounder of Uber and StumbleUpon; Hooman Radfar, founder of AddThis; and Milun Tesovic, founder of Metrolyrics, Expa will invest anywhere from $250,000 to $2 million in the early-stage companies it builds. Many of the ideas and products that come out of Expa emerge organically, as a natural product of bringing together incredible innovators and designers into one space and giving them the time and tools to ideate. Companies they've cobuilt include everything from Sleeperbot, a messaging app for sports fans, to Haus, an open platform for buying and selling homes. "It's not the same playbook every time," Naveen says. "There are multiple ways that ideas and founding teams come together. What matters is, 'Did we figure out an interesting problem? and 'Did we figure out an interesting solution?'"

With offices in New York, San Francisco, and Vancouver, Expa is truly a global company that operates a bit like an extended family. "Everyone stays together," Naveen says. "Once you try something, you can come back into the studio to try the next thing. Alumni come back and work on other things, bringing with them even more talent and other entrepreneurs and founders."

[Apply to] **hello@expa.com**

[Links] Web: **expa.com** Twitter: **@expa** Instagram: **expa**

- **Align your values.**
  Growth, guts, resilience, openness, collaboration and gratitude. This is what it takes to be human, and demonstrating these values – the core values of Human Ventures – is a great way to catch our attention.

- **Fit the profile.**
  We look for three "personas": the serial entrepreneur (you've already had some success and are ready to start the next company); the entrepreneur in corporate clothing (you have unique business insights but the corporate environment is not fulfilling); or the person behind the person (you've been in a high-growth company before and know what you'd do differently next time).

- **Have an idea of what you want to do.**
  We work with founders before they have a pitch deck, before they have a company really fleshed out, so we'll bring in founders when they really know the space that they're interested in.

[Name]

Human Ventures

[Elevator Pitch]

"We're an early-stage venture fund and company builder in New York City. We back and build industry-changing businesses and cofound companies alongside exceptional entrepreneurs."

[Sector] Multiple

[Description]

Investing money can be an impersonal, purely bottom-line business, but one venture fund wants to make this process just a bit more, well, human. Human Ventures, a startup studio in the heart of New York City, is not your average venture capital fund; it's making sure that technology works for humans and not the other way around. "Our early-stage strategy is to be more than just capital," says Heather Hartnett, CEO and founding partner of Human Ventures. "We work with founders from the very beginning to get from startup concept to reality."

For Heather and cofounder Joe Marchese, investing in the next great idea means finding the next good person to come up with it. "A good human means that they're intrinsically good," Heather says. "They're doing good things in the world, and they're also really ambitious." Once selected, these founders work closely alongside the Human Ventures team – made up of domain experts, technologists, entrepreneurs, engineers and designers – to complete a series of one-hundred-day sprints during which they come up with, refine, test and finally market their idea. The goal, Heather says, is to design a product that democratizes access to premium experiences and technologies.

Since it was founded in 2015, Human Ventures has invested in seventeen companies, with the average investment ranging between $500,000 and $1 million. These companies include everything from Current.com, a smart debit card for teens, to Girlboss Media, a media company created by and for women. In all, Human Ventures will cobuild six to ten companies each year, and invest in another ten. These entrepreneurs-in-residence work out of Human Ventures' fourteen-thousand-square-foot location in Manhattan, which also hosts networking events such as Happy Human Hours and generally aims to bring together like-minded individuals who are passionate about solving some of the world's greatest challenges. "The next generation of investment really happens around an ecosystem," Heather says. "Fortune favors the connected."

[Apply to] **humanventures.co**

[Links] Web: **humanventures.co** Twitter: **@Human_Ventures** Instagram: **Humaninthewild**

- **Come up with the next big idea.**
  We're looking for companies that have a really compelling, big idea – an idea that goes beyond just New York: something that can be created here and deployed everywhere.

- **Timing is everything.**
  You have to convince us that now is a good time to deploy your idea.

- **Focus on teams, not founders.**
  Once we feel confident about the idea and timing, we spend our time advising the founding team. They must develop complementary skills and demonstrate grit and perseverance as they build their company.

- **Be early-stage.**
  We specialize in investing in promising companies at the seed level, and taking them to a successful Series A with a top-tier venture capital fund.

[Name]

Lerer Hippeau

[Elevator Pitch] *"We're the most active early-stage venture fund in New York that primarily invests in New York-based companies. We are consistently seed-first investors, and we are consistently New York's first investors."*

[Sector] **Multiple**

[Description] Warby Parker, Everlane, Group Nine Media, Buzzfeed, Namely, Casper, Glossier, Doctor on Demand, Refinery29, Giphy: you name it, chances are Lerer Hippeau has invested in it. Managed by Ken Lerer, Ben Lerer, Eric Hippeau, and Graham Brown, Lerer Hippeau has invested in more than 250 companies with a typical investment ranging from $1 million to $1.5 million. "We've been able to build a brand that's synonymous with early-stage investing in New York," says Eric, managing partner at Lerer Hippeau. "We're very collaborative, so we build a very substantial pipeline of startup opportunities."

Founded in 2010, the firm began as a side project. Eric, then a managing partner at Softbank Capital, met Ken, who cofounded *The Huffington Post*, when he led the digital publisher's Series A. After selling *The Huffington Post*, Eric, Ben and Ken turned their full attention to building Lerer Hippeau. Since the beginning, they've focused on investing in what the city does best. "Because we are primarily investing in New York-based companies," says Eric, "we're a reflection of what New York is good at: software-driven, open-sourced, cloud-based, easy-to-deploy applications and services."

Its growth since then has been tremendous. With a portfolio of more than 250 companies and six early-stage funds – the most recent totaling $122 million – Lerer Hippeau is more than just an early-stage investor. The company also raised $60 million for its second "Select Fund," which is designed for follow-on investment in companies that are raising Series A and Series B rounds. It offers a variety of tools, including a platform team and a full-time recruiter. "All of us have an operating background, so we're very operations conscious," Eric says. "We spend a lot of time on strategy, and we make sure we're all in agreement as to the kind of metrics that teams need."

[Apply to] **No online applications. Find someone in their network for an introduction and reference.**

[Links] Web: **lererhippeau.com** Facebook: **LererHippeau** Twitter: **@LererHippeau** Instagram: **lererhippeau**

- **Have a great leader.**
  About two hundred companies apply each month, and every individual investor makes their decision based on their own rubric, but in general our members are looking for companies that have amazing founders. You can define "amazing" however you'd like, but what it comes down to is we're looking for people who we believe can, simply, figure it out.

- **Be scalable.**
  Second to "Can they figure it out?" is "Can they scale their business?"

- **Be coachable.**
  If you want to be coached, be coachable. The mentality among many of the startups in New York is that they want to be coached. Have a "challenge me" mentality.

- **Can the company exit?**
  The only way you get a return on your investment is through an acquisition or a very rare IPO. So we ask, can we imagine this company being one that gets acquired down the line?

[Name]

New York Angels

[Elevator Pitch] *"We're the oldest and largest general angel group in New York City. Our members are generally successful in their previous work, and look to be smart, professional-level investors in companies that can produce a quality return for the entrepreneur and investor."*

[Sector] **Multiple**

[Description] "Angel investing is a contact sport," says Brian Cohen, chairman at New York Angels. "If you're an angel investor, you want the joy, you want the intrigue of being one-on-one with founders to make investing decisions yourself." And if you're a startup, you definitely want Cohen, or one of the other 130 New York Angels members, on your side to help you grow your business.

New York Angels is New York City's oldest and largest angel group. It's not an angel fund, which makes decisions as a unit, but a coalition of like-minded investors from a multitude of backgrounds who individually invest anywhere from $25,000 to $1.5 million in early-stage startups. Members have led or participated in seed investment rounds in companies from Pinterest to JUMP Bikes and invested in twenty companies that have successfully exited the market. Overall, the group has invested more than $150 million in over two hundred companies.

New York Angels are never passive investors but rather provide mentoring, networking opportunities and business assistance to the founders they work with. Investors come from all walks of life, from entrepreneurship to finance, and get together on a regular basis for discovery, due diligence and breakfast meetings. "It's a fast-paced, fast-moving organization," says Cohen. "Our primary interest is the success of the entrepreneur."

For New York Angels members, angel investing is not a game but a serious business. From entrepreneurship demo days to the thriving New York City startup scene, members are always engaging with the community. "We view what we do as an honor," says Cohen. "From medical devices, new social networks and voice-input technologies, to a whole host of what may be on the fringe of brain technology or Bitcoin technology, it's the most fun you can have while being serious about making an opportunistic investment."

[Apply to] **newyorkangels.com**

[Links] Web: **newyorkangels.com** Twitter: **@theNYangels** LinkedIn: **company/new-york-angels**

- **Let us see your experience.**
  We look for strong teams that have some domain experience, sales and marketing expertise, and prior startup experience. We ask, “Why are you uniquely positioned to build this business?”

- **Have a solid business model and business plan.**
  What we want to know is “Can this company get to an inflection point?”

- **Ensure you have a product-market fit.**
  Does your company have something that’s ten times better than what currently exists? Do you have something customers love?

- **Be able to grow.**
  We’re looking for companies that can knock out the competition and continue to expand. What’s the size of the market, and can the company fit in it? Are there hundreds of competitors or dozens of competitors?

[Name]

RRE Ventures

[Elevator Pitch]

"We provide expertise, resources and networks to help early-stage founders navigate the challenges of building and growing an innovative company. We've been investing in great teams for twenty-four years and are excited to continue backing the next generation of founders."

[Sector]

Enterprise software, financial services, blockchain/crypto, media, robotics, VR/AR, space and satellites, AI/ML, real estate technology, consumer and healthcare IT

[Description]

When it comes to investing in the New York City startup ecosystem, RRE Ventures is the godfather, of sorts. Founded in 1994 by James D. Robinson III, James D. Robinson IV and Stuart Ellman, RRE has raised an estimated $1.7 billion across seven funds to invest in early-stage companies and one opportunity fund to support the growth of their portfolio. Typically, RRE Ventures invests in seed companies (generally around $300,000) and Series A and B (with check size ranging from $1 million to $7 million). These investments have led to more than sixty acquisitions and seventeen IPOs, including in companies such as *Business Insider*, Venmo, and *The Huffington Post*. Unlike some of the newer VC funds, RRE Ventures has been there for the good and the bad – and survived. "Our longevity means that we've been through up-cycles and down-cycles," says Will Porteous, general partner and COO. "It isn't always rosy, but some of the value that we create here is that we know how to manage through the down-cycles."

RRE Ventures doesn't just invest in companies; it also plays a role in providing new companies with business development, talent development and community learning opportunities while also serving on company boards throughout the lifecycle of the company. In addition, it connects startups with Fortune 500 companies across expertise areas from financial services to healthcare, advertising and media.

For RRE Ventures, the game may have changed since the mid-1990s, but the vision remains the same. "When we started back in the nineties, it was connecting the dots between the technologies of the future and the corporations of the present," says Maria Palma, vice president of business development. "We've seen that the talent pool has gotten more robust, the cost of starting a business has gone down, and the sheer diversity of industry and people here have created the grounds for a flourishing tech ecosystem. We see that continuing going forward."

[Apply to] rre.com/team or info@rre.com

[Links] Web: rre.com Facebook: RREVC Twitter: @RRE Instagram: rreventures

- **Fit within our thesis.**
  We try to be very precise about what we're interested in, and then to see relatively few companies.

- **Reach out.**
  We're incredibly reachable. Many of us blog and are active on Twitter. We're very clear about the kinds of things we're interested in, and we respond to cold emails all the time when they're high-quality cold emails.

- **Show conviction.**
  We have to have a sense that founders have genuine conviction about what they're doing, and that they're in it for the right reasons.

- **Be curious.**
  Our founders and companies are intellectually curious, have a growth mindset, and want to learn. We don't look for things like having graduated from a specific school. We work with a lot of first time entrepreneurs from a wide variety of backgrounds.

[Name]

Union Square Ventures

[Elevator Pitch]

"We're a New York–based venture capital firm. We back trusted brands that broaden access to knowledge, capital and well-being by leveraging networks, platforms and protocols."

[Sector]

Multiple

[Description]

Whether it's adding an Opportunity Fund, developing a network among its portfolio companies, or being one of the first VC funds to invest in blockchain, Union Square Ventures (USV) is always taking a look in the mirror to see what it can do better, and then doing it. Perhaps that's why it's one of New York's most successful VC firms. It's now investing from its fifth fund (along with a parallel Opportunity Fund) and has an active portfolio of over seventy-five companies. USV has invested in companies whose exits are worth billions of dollars in total, including industry-changing companies such as Twitter, Etsy and Twilio. "We're constantly questioning what we're doing and how we're doing it," says Albert Wenger, managing partner at USV. "We have an overarching investment thesis, and within that we develop specific ideas of what we're looking for."

That quest for self-improvement complements USV's thesis-driven model. As opposed to deal flow–driven investing, where VC funds will meet as many companies as possible, thesis-driven investors are more selective and pro-active, often seeking out companies. USV is now on its third thesis, which looks for companies and projects that broaden access to knowledge (e.g., Duolingo), capital (e.g., Stash), and well-being (e.g., Clue). USV also looks for companies whose business models align incentives with end users. "Only if your incentives are aligned with the users of your product or service will you be able to build a trusted brand," says Albert.

USV, founded in 2003 by Brad Burnham and Fred Wilson, will typically invest anywhere from $1 million in early stage companies to $15 million in growth companies. It also invests in later-stage companies (via its Opportunity Fund). Beyond investing, USV connects to its companies to broader networking opportunities. "We're focused on building infrastructure that helps connect people at USV portfolio companies to each other," Albert says. "When someone joins one of our portfolio companies, they're also joining a seven-thousand-person-strong network of experts."

[Apply to]

usv.com

[Links]

Web: **usv.com** Twitter: **@usv**

- **Be passionate about problems.**
  We're looking for really great teams who are enraptured by the problem they're solving.

- **Let us help you.**
  From a timing perspective, we look for things like, "Do we think we can have a material impact on the trajectory of your company over the course of five months?"

- **Build local, think global.**
  Companies should be looking at opportunities that are global in nature and that ultimately can really improve life in cities.

- **Assemble a great team.**
  We look for team members who have a growth mindset, who are intentional about their culture, who want to learn, and who can run experiments quickly for venture-scale opportunities.

[Name]

URBAN-X

[Elevator Pitch]

"We're an accelerator for startups that are reinventing city life. We invest in technology companies working in areas like mobility, energy, real estate tech, food tech and ultimately anything that builds more efficient and more livable cities."

[Sector]

Multiple

[Description]

"The key thing is not to fall in love with your solution but to fall in love with the problem," says Micah Kotch, managing director at URBAN-X, a five-month accelerator program that helps startups address critical city challenges. And in cities across the country and around the world, there is no shortage of problems. From finding ways to reduce traffic to dealing with trash collection or addressing rising rents and displacement, cities are always seeking to become fairer, more efficient and, well, smarter. That's where URBAN-X comes in.

Founded as a partnership between the car company MINI and Urban Us, the world's first VC firm focused on cities, URBAN-X invests $100,000 in early-stage companies through Series A over the course of a fourteen-week intensive accelerator program. Since its founding, URBAN-X has invested in thirty companies. These generally fall into seven broad categories: built environment and real estate; infrastructure and industry; food, waste and water; public health and safety; energy and grid; govtech and civic solutions; and transportation and mobility. The startups have included everything from a company that uses AI to monitor and manage roadways (Roadbotics) to a startup that offers responsive, intelligent bike helmets for commuters (Brooklyness). "We started this program really looking to engage with entrepreneurs who are developing solutions to society-scale problems," Micah says.

URBAN-X is by no means a passive investor. Founders work closely with an in-house team of resident experts who help startups with product design, UX/UI software development and mechanical and electrical engineering, to name just a few things. After they complete the five-month program, they're also able to receive additional funding through Urban Us and BMW iVentures follow-on funds. "Whether our companies have a hardware or software solution," says Micah, "we work actively with them to help them build their product with the best-in-class development and design resources."

[Apply to] **urban-x.com/apply**

[Links] Web: **urban-x.com** Facebook: **urbanxaccel** Twitter: **@urbanxaccel** Instagram: **urbanxaccel**

directory

Startups

ConsenSys
consensys.net

Ellevest
48 West 25th Street, 6th Floor
New York 10010
ellevest.com

Farmshelf
19 Morris Avenue, Building 128
Brooklyn 11205
farmshelf.com

Handy
53 West 23rd Street, 3rd Floor
New York 10010
handy.com

Justworks
601 West 26th Street, 4th Floor
New York 10001
justworks.com

Lemonade Insurance Company
5 Crosby Street, 3rd Floor
New York 10013
lemonade.com

Managed by Q
233 Spring Street, 11th Floor East
New York 10013
managedbyq.com

Propel
147 Prince Street,
Brooklyn 11201
joinpropel.com

x.ai
200 Broadway, Level 3
New York 10038
x.ai

Programs

Blue Ridge Labs @ Robin Hood
150 Court Street, 2nd Floor
Brooklyn 11201
labs.robinhood.org

Entrepreneurs Roundtable Accelerator
415 Madison Avenue, 4th Floor
New York 10017
eranyc.com

Founder Institute
261 5th Avenue
New York 10016
fi.co

Fullstack Academy
5 Hanover Square, 11th Floor
New York 10004
fullstackacademy.com

General Assembly New York (Manhattan)
Classrooms
10 East 21st Street
New York 10010
generalassemb.ly

Grand Central Tech
335 Madison Ave
New York, NY 10017
company.co

New York Tech Alliance
c/o Civic Hall
118 West 22nd Street
New York 10011
nytech.org

NYC Media Lab
2 Metrotech Center
Brooklyn 11201
nycmedialab.org

NYC Open Data
opendata.cityofnewyork.us

NYU Tandon Future Labs
137 Varick Street, 2nd Floor
New York 10013
futurelabs.nyc

Per Scholas
804 East 138th Street
Bronx 10454
perscholas.org

She Innovates Global Program / UN Women
220 East 42nd Street
New York 10017
unwomen.org

Spaces

The Assemblage
114 East 25th Street
New York 10015
theassemblage.com

Bond Collective
55 Broadway, 3rd Floor
New York 10006
bondcollective.com

Civic Hall
118 West 22nd Street, 12th Floor
New York 10011
civichall.org

New Lab
19 Morris Avenue,
Building 128, Cumberland Gate
Brooklyn 11205
newlab.com

Pencilworks
61 Greenpoint Avenue, 6th Floor
Brooklyn 11222
pencilwork.com

SAP Next-Gen
10 Hudson Yards, 48th Floor
New York 10001
sap.com/next-gen

Urban Tech Hub at Company
335 Madison Avenue, Floor 4
New York 10017
hubatgct.com

WeWork
115 West 18th Street
New York 10011
wework.com

The Yard HQ
510 Fifth Ave, 3rd Floor
New York 10036
theyard.com

Experts

BerlinRosen
15 Maiden Lane
Suite 1600
New York 10038
berlinrosen.com

Flying Saucer Studio
flyingsaucer.nyc

Kickstarter
Greenpoint, Brooklyn
kickstarter.com

SAP Next-Gen / SAP Leonardo Center New York
10 Hudson Yards
New York 10001
sap.com/next-gen

Founders

AlleyCorp
229 West 43rd Street, 5th Floor
New York 10036
alleycorp.com

Kargo
826 Broadway, 5th Floor
New York 10003
kargo.com

NYU Tandon Future Labs
137 Varick Street, 2nd Floor
New York, NY 10013
futurelabs.nyc

Silicon Harlem
8 West 126th Street, 3rd Floor
New York 10027
siliconharlem.net

Sprinklr
29 West 35th Street, 7th Floor
New York 10001
sprinklr.com

VentureOut
25 West 39th Street, 14th Floor
New York 10018
ventureoutny.com

WayUp
114 W 26th St
New York, NY 10001
wayup.com

Zola
150 Broadway, 19th Floor
New York, NY 10038
zola.com

Schools

Columbia Entrepreneurship
535 West 116 Street
New York 10027
entrepreneurship.columbia.edu

Cooper Union
30 Cooper Square
New York 10003
cooper.edu/welcome

Cornell Tech
2 West Loop Road,
New York, NY 10044
tech.cornell.edu

Fordham University, Lincoln Center
33 West 60th Street
New York 10023
fordham.edu

The New School
66 West 12th Street
New York 10011
newschool.edu

Investors

BBG Ventures
770 Broadway, 5th Floor
New York 10003
bbgventures.com

Brooklyn Bridge Ventures
55-C 9th Street
Brooklyn 11215
brooklynbridge.vc

Expa
expa.com

Human Ventures
386 Park Avenue South, 5th Floor
New York 10016
humanventures.co

Lerer Hippeau
100 Crosby Street, Suite 308
New York 10012
lererhippeau.com

New York Angels
1216 Broadway, 2nd Floor
New York 10001
newyorkangels.com

RRE Ventures
130 East 59th Street, 17th Floor
New York 10022
rre.com

Union Square Ventures
915 Broadway, 19th Floor
New York 10010
usv.com

URBAN-X (at A/D/O)
29 Norman Avenue
Brooklyn 11222
urban-x.com

directory

Accountants

CohnReznick LLP
1301 Avenue of the Americas
New York 10019
cohnreznick.com

Countsy
countsy.com

Dave Burton, CPA
85 Broad St., 17th Fl
New York 10004
daveburton.nyc

Early Growth Financial Services
33 Irving Place
New York 10003
earlygrowthfinancialservices.com

EisnerAmper
750 3rd Avenue
New York 10017
eisneramper.com/new-york-city-ny

Escalon
59 East 54 Street, Suite 72
New York 10022
escalon.services

KPMG
345 Park Ave
New York 10154
kpmg.com

Kruze Consulting
145 West 30th Street 7th Floor
New York 10001
kruzeconsulting.com/new_york_city

Nezaj & Co
1030 Morris Park Avenue
Bronx 10461
nezajcpa.com

Nomad Financial
119 West 24th Street, 4th Floor
New York 10011
nomadfinancial.com

PricewaterhouseCoopers
300 Madison Avenue
New York 10017
pwc.com

Propeller Industries
110 William Street, Suite 2200
New York 10038
propellerindustries.com

Withum Audit Tax Advisory
1411 Broadway, 23rd Floor
New York 10018
withum.com

Banks

Azlo
azlo.com

Capital One
299 Park Ave
New York 10017
capitalone.com

First Republic
443 Park Avenue South
New York 10016
firstrepublic.com

HSBC
425 5th Avenue
New York 10018
us.hsbc.com

Santander Bank
45 East 53rd Street
New York 10022
santanderbank.com/us/personal

Silicon Valley Bank
387 Park Avenue South, 2nd Floor
New York 10016
svb.com/new-york

Square 1 Bank
475 5th Avenue, 18th Floor
New York 10017
square1bank.com

U.S. Bank
461 5th Avenue
New York 10017
usbank.com/index.html

Coffee Shops and Places with Wifi

Ace Hotel, New York
20 W 29th St, New York, NY 10001, USA
www.acehotel.com/newyork

Astoria Coffee
30-04 30th Street, Astoria
New York 11102
astoriacoffeeny.com

Birch Coffee
21 East 27th Street
New York 10016
birchcoffee.com

Black Fox Coffee Co.
70 Pine Street
New York 10005
blackfoxcoffee.com

Blank Slate
121 Madison Avenue
New York 10016
blankslatenyc.com

Bluestone Lane
55 Prospect Street
Brooklyn 11201
bluestonelane.com/coffee-shops

Boogie Down Grind Café
866 Hunts Point Avenue
Bronx 10474
boogiedowngrindcafe.com

Brooklyn Roasting Company
50 West 23rd Street
New York 10010
brooklynroasting.com

Cafe Grumpy
193 Meserole Avenue
Brooklyn 11222
cafegrumpy.com

Culture Espresso
72 West 38th Street
New York 10018
cultureespresso.com

Devoción
69 Grand Street
Brooklyn 11249
devocion.com

Double Dutch Espresso
2430 3rd Avenue
Bronx 10451
doubledutchespresso.com

Freehold
45 South 3rd Street
Brooklyn 11249
freeholdbrooklyn.com

Ground Support Cafe
399 West Broadway
New York 10012
groundsupportcafe.com

Grounded
28 Jane Street
New York 10014
groundedcoffee.com

Housing Works Bookstore Cafe
126 Crosby Street
New York 10012
housingworks.org/locations/bookstore-cafe

Ludlow Coffee Supply
176 Ludlow Street
New York 10002
ludlowcoffeesupply.com

Perk Kafe
162 East 37th St
New York 10016
perkkafe.com

Ramini Espresso Bar
265 West 37th Street
New York 10018
ramininyc.com

Roger Smith Hotel
501 Lexington Ave, New York, NY 10017, USA
www.rogersmith.com

Sweetleaf
10-93 Jackson Avenue
Long Island City 11101
sweetleafcoffee.com

Stumptown Coffee Roasters
418 West 29th Street
New York 10001
stumptowncoffee.com/locations/newyork

Taylor St. Baristas
33 East 40th Street
New York 10016
taylor-st.com/pages/new-york

Think Coffee
248 Mercer Street
New York 10012
thinkcoffee.com

Toby's Estate Coffee
125 North 6th Street
Brooklyn 11249
tobysestate.com

Variety Coffee Roasters
368 Graham Ave
Brooklyn 11211
varietycoffeeroasters.com

Flats and Rentals

Citi Habitats
citihabitats.com

Compass
compass.com

Common
common.com

Naked Apartments
nakedapartments.com

Nooklyn
nooklyn.com

RentHop
renthop.com

Roomi
roomiapp.com

StreetEasy
streeteasy.com

WeLive
welive.com

Zillow
zillow.com/browse/homes/ny

Important Government Offices

NYC Business
110 William Street, 7th Floor
New York 10038
nyc.gov/nycbusiness

NYC Department of Information Technology and Telecommunications
2 MetroTech Center, 5th Floor
Brooklyn 11201
www1.nyc.gov/site/doitt/index.page

NYC Economic Development Corporation
110 William Street
New York 10038
nycedc.com

NYC Mayor's Office of the Chief Technology Officer
11 Centre Street
New York 10007
tech.cityofnewyork.us

NYC Small Business Services
110 William Street, 7th Floor
New York 10038
www1.nyc.gov/site/sbs/index.page

U.S. Citizenship and Immigration Services
26 Federal Plaza, 3rd Floor, Room 3-120
New York 10278
uscis.gov/about-us/find-uscis-office/field-offices/new-york-new-york-field-office

directory

Incubators and Accelerators

AngelPad
angelpad.org

Betaworks
29 Little West 12th Street
New York 10014
betaworks.com

Blueprint Health
447 Broadway
New York 10013
blueprinthealth.org

Capital One Labs
114 5th Avenue
New York 10011
capitalonelabs.com

CUNY Startup Accelerator
55 Lexington Avenue, 2nd Floor
New York 10010
cunystartups.com/accelerator

Dreamit Ventures
33 Irving Place, 10th Floor
New York 10003
dreamit.com

Fashion Tech Consortium
25 West 39th Street
New York 10018
fashiontechco.com

Founder Institute
261 5th Avenue
New York 10016
fi.co/s/new_york

MetaBronx
208 Rider Avenue
Bronx 10451
metabronx.com

MetaProp NYC
18 W 21st Street
New York 10010
metaprop.org

New York Fashion Tech Lab
6 St. Johns Lane
New York 10013
nyftlab.com

Prehype
221 Canal St
New York 10013
prehype.com

Quake Capital
85 Broad St
New York 10004
quakecapital.com

Starters
350 5th Ave, 76th Floor
New York 10118
starters.co

Tata Innovation Center
11 East Loop Rd
New York 10044
tech.cornell.edu/campus/ta-ta-innovation-center

Tech Incubator at Queens College
65–30 Kissena Blvd.
Queens 11367
tiqc.nyc

Techstars NYC
techstars.com/nyc-program

WeWork Labs
81 Prospect St
Brooklyn 11201
wework.com/labs

Work-Bench
110 5th Avenue, 5th Floor
New York 10011
work-bench.com

Zahn Innovation Center
160 Convent Ave
New York 10031
zahncenternyc.com

Insurance Companies

Aetna
100 Park Ave #12
New York 10017
aetna.com

Affinity Health Plan
1776 Eastchester Road
Bronx 10461
affinityplan.org

Blue Cross Blue Shield
15 Metrotech Ctr Brooklyn
Brooklyn 11201
empireblue.com

Chubb Insurance
1133 Avenue of the Americas
New York 10036
chubb.com

Founder Shield
119 West 24th Street, 4th Floor
New York 10011
foundershield.com

Health First
100 Church Street
New York 10007
healthfirst.org

La Playa Insurance
175 Varick Street, 8th Floor
New York 10014
laplayainsurance.com

Lockton
1185 Avenue of the Americas,
Suite 2010
New York 10036
lockton.com/offices/new-york

Metroplus
160 Water Street #3
New York 10038
metroplus.org

New York Life Insurance Company
51 Madison Avenue
New York 10010
newyorklife.com

Oscar
295 Lafayette Street
New York 10012
hioscar.com/ny

P&G Insurance Brokers, Inc.
3923 Fort Hamilton Parkway
Brooklyn 11218
pandginsurance.com

Language Schools

ABC Languages
146 W 29th Street, 6th Floor
New York 10001
abclang.com

Be Fluent NYC
15 West 39th Street, 11th Floor
New York 10018
befluentnyc.com

Fluent City
330 5th Avenue, #8
New York 10001
fluentcity.com/language/new-york

City Speakeasy
226 West 37th Street, 11th Floor
New York 10018
cityspeakeasy.com

Hills Learning
50 East 42nd Street, #900
New York 10017
hillslearning.com

Idlewild Books
170 7th Avenue South
New York 10014
idlewildbooks.com

Kaplan International
63rd Floor, 350 5th Ave
New York 10118
kaplaninternational.com

Rennert International
211 East 43rd Street, 2nd Floor
New York 10017
rennert.com

Legal

Dentons
1221 Avenue of the Americas
New York 10020-1089
dentons.com

Mccarter & English Worldwide Plaza
825 Eighth Avenue, 31st Floor
New York 10019
mccarter.com

Cooley
The Grace Building
1114 Avenue of the Americas, 46th Floor
New York 10036-7798
cooley.com/about/offices/new-york

LawTrades
lawtrades.com

Sheppard Mullin
30 Rockefeller Plaza
New York 10112
sheppardmullin.com/new-york

Gray
119 West 24th Street, 4th Floor
New York 10011
gray.legal

Startup Events

AlleyWatch
events.alleywatch.com/nyc-tech-startup-events/

Built In NYC
builtinnyc.com/events

Civic Hall
civichall.org/eventscal/

Cornell Tech at Bloomberg
bloombergtalks.com

Digital.NYC
digital.nyc/events

Eventbrite
eventbrite.com/d/ny--new-york/startup-event/

Gary's Guide
garysguide.com/events

General Assembly Events
generalassemb.ly

Meetup
meetup.com

Shapr
shapr.co

Startup Grind New York
startupgrind.com/new-york

Tech Day New York
techdayhq.com/new-york

glossary

A

Accelerator
An organization or program that offers advice and resources to help small businesses grow

Acqui-hire
Buying out a company based on the skills of its staff rather than its service or product

Angel Investment
Outside funding with shared ownership equity

API
Application programming interface

ARR
Accounting (or average) rate of return: calculation generated from net income of the proposed capital investment

Artificial Intelligence
The simulation of human intelligence by computer systems; machines that are able to perform tasks normally carried out by humans

B2B
(Business-to-Business)
The exchange of services, information and/or products from a business to a business

B2C
(Business-to-Consumer)
The exchange of services, information and/or products from a business to a consumer

Blockchain
A digital and public collection of financial accounts for all cryptocurrency transactions

BOM
(Bill of Materials)
A list of the parts or components required to build a product

Bootstrap
To self-fund, without outside investment

Bridge Loan
A loan taken out for a short-term period, typically between two weeks and three years, until long-term financing can be organized

Burn Rate
The amount of money a startup spends

Business Angel
An experienced entrepreneur or professional who provides starting or growth capital for promising startups

Business Model Canvas
A template that gives a coherent overview of the key drivers of a business in order to bring innovation into current or new business models

C

C-level
Chief position

Cap Table
An analysis of ownership stakes in a company

CMO
Chief marketing officer

Cold-Calling
The solicitation of potential customers who had no prior interaction with the solicitor

Convertible Note/Loan
A type of short-term debt often used by seed investors to delay establishing a valuation for the startup until a later round of funding or milestone

Coworking
A shared working environment

CPA
Cost per action

CPC
Cost per click

Cybersecurity
Technologies, processes and practices designed to protect against the criminal or unauthorized use of electronic data

D

Dealflow
Term for investors that refers to the rate at which they receive potential business deals

Deeptech
Companies founded on the discoveries or innovations of technologists and scientists

Diluting
A reduction in the ownership percentage of a share of stock due to new equity shares being issued

E

Elevator Pitch
A short summary used to quickly define a product or idea

Ethereum
A blockchain-based software platform and programming language that helps developers build and publish distributed applications

Exit
A way to transition the ownership of a company to another company

F

Fintech
Financial technology

Flex Desk
Shared desk in a space where coworkers are free to move around and sit wherever they like

I

Incubator
Facility established to nurture young startup firms during their first few months or years of development

Installed Base
The number of units of a certain type of product that have been sold and are actually being used

IP
(Intellectual Property)
Property which is not tangible; the result of creativity, such as patents and copyrights

IPO
(Initial Public Offering)
The first time a company's stock is offered for sale to the public

K

KPI
(Key Performance Indicator)
A value that is measurable and demonstrates how effectively a company is achieving key business objectives

L

Later-Stage
More mature startups/companies

Lean
Refers to 'lean startup methodology;' the method proposed by Eric Ries in his book for developing businesses and startups through product development cycles

Lean LaunchPad
A methodology for entrepreneurs to test and develop business models based on inquiring with and learning from customers

M

M&A
(Mergers and Acquisitions)
A merger is when two companies join to form a new company, while an acquisition is the purchase of one company by another where no new company is formed

MAU
Monthly active user

MVP
Minimum viable product

O

Opportunities Fund
Investment in companies or sectors in areas where growth opportunities are anticipated

P

P2P
(Peer-to-Peer)
A network created when two or more PCs are connected and sharing resources without going through a separate server

glossary

Pitch Deck
A short version of a business plan presenting key figures generally to investors

PR Kit (Press Kit)
Package of promotional materials, such as pictures, logos and descriptions of a company

Product-Market Fit
When a product has created significant customer value and its best target industries have been identified

Pro-market
A market economy/a capitalistic economy

S

SaaS
Software as a service

Scaleup
A company that has already validated its product in a market and is economically sustainable

Seed Funding
First round, small, early-stage investment from family members, friends, banks or an investor

Seed Investor
An investor focusing on the seed round

Seed Round
The first round of funding

Series A/B/C/D
The name of funding rounds that come after the seed stage

Shares
Units of ownership of a company that belong to a shareholder

Solopreneurs
A person who sets up and runs a business on their own and typically does not hire employees

Startup
Companies under three years old, in the growth stage and becoming profitable (if not already)

SVP
Senior Vice President

T

Term Sheet/Letter of Intent
The document between an investor and a startup including the conditions for financing (commonly non-binding)

U

Unicorn
A company often in the tech or software sector worth over US$1 billion

USP
Unique selling point

UX
(User experience design) The process of designing and improving user satisfaction with products so that they are useful, easy to use and pleasurable to interact with

V

VC
(Venture Capital) Financing from a pool of investors in a venture capital firm in return for equity

Vesting
Process that involves giving or earning a right to a present or future payment, benefit or asset

Z

Zebras
Companies which aim for sustainable prosperity and are powered by people who work together to create change beyond a positive financial return

DUNKIN' DONUTS
STELLA ARTOIS
LIVE
IN WITH THE NEW
COMING SOON
FJALL RAVEN
ROCKETTES.COM
NYPD
OPEN

→ startupguide.com

Follow us   

About the Guide

Based on traditional guidebooks that can be carried around everywhere, Startup Guide books help you navigate and connect with different startup scenes across the globe. Each book is packed with useful information, exciting entrepreneur stories and insightful interviews with local experts. We hope the book will become your trusted companion as you embark on a new (startup) journey. Today, Startup Guide books are in seventeen different cities in Europe, the US and the Middle East, including Berlin, London, New York, Tel Aviv, Stockholm, Copenhagen, Vienna, Lisbon and Paris.

How we make the guides:
To ensure an accurate and trustworthy guide every time, we team up with a city partner that is established in the local startup scene. We then ask the local community to nominate startups, coworking spaces, founders, schools, investors, incubators and established businesses to be featured through an online submission form. Based on the results, these submissions are narrowed down to the top hundred organizations and individuals. Next, the local advisory board – which is selected by our community partner and consists of key players in the local startup community – votes for the final selection, ensuring a balanced representation of industries and startup stories in each book. The local community partner then works in close collaboration with our international editorial and design team to help research, organize interviews with journalists as well as plan photoshoots with photographers. Finally, all content is reviewed, edited and put into the book's layout by the Startup Guide team in Berlin and Lisbon before going for print in Berlin.

Where to find us: The easiest way to get your hands on a Startup Guide book is to order it from our online shop: startupguide.com/shop

If you prefer to do things in real life, drop by one of the fine retailers listed on the stockists page on our website.

Want to become a stockist or suggest a store?

Get in touch here:
sales@startupguide.com

STARTUP
GUIDE
STORE

The Startup Guide Stores

Whether it's sniffing freshly printed books or holding an innovative product, we're huge fans of physical experiences. That's why we opened two stores – one in Lisbon and another in Berlin. Not only do the stores showcase our books and curated products, they're also our offices and a place for the community to come together to share wows and hows. Say hello!

Lisbon:
R. Rodrigues de Faria 103
Edifício G6, 1300 - 501 Lisboa
Tue-Sun: 12h-19h
+351 21 139 8791
lisbon@startupguide.com

Berlin:
Waldemarstraße 38, 10999 Berlin
Mon-Fri: 10h-18h
+49 (0)30-37468679
berlin@startupguide.com

#startupeverywhere

Startup Guide is a creative content and publishing company founded by Sissel Hansen in 2014. We produce guidebooks and tools to help entrepreneurs navigate and connect with different startup scenes across the globe. As the world of work changes, our mission is to guide, empower and inspire people to start their own business anywhere. Today, Startup Guide books are in 17 different cities in Europe, the US and the Middle East, including Berlin, London, Tel Aviv, Stockholm, Copenhagen, Vienna, Lisbon and Paris. We also have two physical stores in Berlin and Lisbon to promote and sell products by startup. Startup Guide is a 20-person team based in Berlin and Lisbon.
Visit our site for more: startupguide.com

Want to get more info, be a partner or say hello?

Shoot us an email here info@startupguide.com

Join us and #startupeverywhere

New York Advisory Board

Aaron N. Block
Cofounder and Managing Director
MetaProp NYC

Alessandra Henderson
Human Ventures AND Founding Executive Director
MIT NYC Startup Studio

Ann Rosenberg
Senior Vice President, Global Head,
SAP Next-Gen
Global Lead,
UN Women #sheinnovates

Ben Christensen
Innovation Manager
SAP Next-Gen

Brian Cohen
Chairman at New York Angels & Founding Partner,
New York Venture Partners

Brian Laung Aoaeh, CFA
Partner
Particle Ventures (Formerly known as KEC Ventures)

Clayton Banks
CEO
Silicon Harlem

Dan Kozikowski
VP of Platform
FirstMark

Daren McKelvey
Founder
R1 Labs

David S. Rose
Founder & CEO
Gust

Julie Samuels
Executive Director
Tech:NYC

Karin Klein
Founding Partner
Bloomberg Beta

Marcos Dinnerstein
Founding Editor
A Better Mousetrap

Maria Palma
Vice President, Business Development / Head of Platform
RRE Ventures

Maria Teresa Cometto
Journalist
Corriere della Sera

Matthew Harrigan
Cofounder and CEO, Company & Managing Director,
Grand Central Tech

Michal Rosenn
General Counsel
Expa

Minerva L Tantoco
Former CTO City of New York
Co-Founder, Grasshopper

Sandra Moerch
Global Head
SAP Next-Gen
Brand & Site Manager
SAP's Purpose Driven Innovation Center

Sarah Brown
Chief of Staff
Tech:NYC

Shaina Horowitz
Urban Tech Hub Director
New Lab

Zach Goldstein
Analyst
Union Square Ventures

John M. Lynn
Cofounder, Creator
The Studio Project + Accelerator Awesome

With thanks to our **Content Partners**

NYCEDC

KICKSTARTER

berlin rosen

New York • Washington, D.C. • Los Angeles

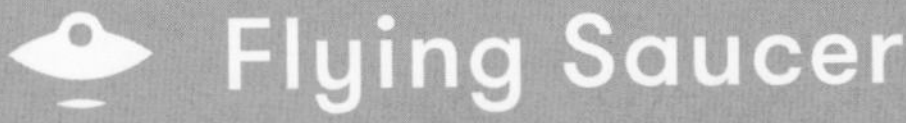

Our **Local Community Partner**

And our **Media Supporters**

SILICON NYC

Hudson Yards / Tech & Innovation Hub

Envisioned to be more than eighteen million square feet of commercial and residential space, Hudson Yards is a glimpse into the future of city living – now. "What marks it as unique is its mixture of community, retail and residential offices, attractions and public spaces that we believe will become a new way of urban living and working for the future," says Jay Cross, President of Hudson Yards. Currently under construction, the first phase of the futuristic neighborhood is scheduled to open in 2019 with the second phase planned to open in 2025.

Startups and entrepreneurs are constantly striving to look for new ways of doing things, so why not live and work in a neighborhood that's as forward-thinking and innovative as the ideas they're coming up with? Hudson Yards, developed by Related Companies and Oxford Properties, will be more than a cluster of skyscrapers and parks; rather, says Jay, all of its buildings, streets, parks and public spaces will be connected by a cutting-edge technology infrastructure that allows the building systems to interact and respond to each other. In essence, it will be a smart neighborhood that harnesses data to create a personalized and smoother experience for everyone – whether a resident, employee or visitor.

Located at the top of the High Line in Manhattan near Hell's Kitchen, Hudson Yards has already attracted a throng of young, educated and ambitious people to its first office building, and many are dubbing it the next tech and innovation hub in New York. It's no surprise, considering innovators like VaynerMedia, SAP, Sidewalk Labs and BCG Digital Ventures have already set up shop at 10 Hudson Yards, with media companies and brands like Warner Bros and Coach plugging into the development. "I think Hudson Yard's combination of new infrastructure and larger buildings is attractive to tech companies that want to grow and, in turn, attract startups," says Jay. "It's becoming a new tech hub for the city."

Visit HudsonYardsNewYork.com for more info.

[Links] Facebook: HudsonYardsNewYork Twitter: @_HudsonYardsNYC Instagram: _hudsonyardsnyc

25

Mayor's Office of the Chief Technology Officer

Jeremy M. Goldberg, Deputy CTO at the Mayor's Office of the CTO

In a city as diverse and fast-moving as New York, ensuring that technological change doesn't leave anyone behind is critical to enabling a fair future for all New Yorkers. But doing this is easier said than done. With its more than 8.5 million residents, a high and rising rate of income inequality, and the encroaching gentrification in many low-income neighborhoods, New York faces significant challenges when it comes to equity – both digital and otherwise.

In this context, technology can either be part of the problem or part of the solution. Finding these solutions is where the New York City Mayor's Office of the Chief Technology Officer (CTO) comes in. An initiative spearheaded by Mayor Bill de Blasio, the Mayor's Office of the CTO runs four main programs – NYC Connected, NYC Digital, NYC Forward, and NYCx – that aim to promote digital equity across the city's five boroughs. "New York City is the largest and most diverse city in the country, made up of a wide variety of people with different needs," says Jeremy M. Goldberg, Deputy CTO at the Mayor's Office of the CTO. "We help facilitate and coordinate engagement with the public, and the ability to leverage our office as a platform to inspire and motivate new ideas and opportunities."

The Office of the CTO is engaged in many projects, from leading NYC Connected, which aims to expand broadband internet access to all New Yorkers by 2025 (in line with Mayor de Blasio's promise), to running NYCx, which brings together community, startups, industry, leading entrepreneurs, and city agencies to tackle challenges in fields ranging from connectivity to public health and climate change. NYCx in particular offers startups and entrepreneurs in the tech space opportunities to develop solutions to city challenges by working directly with neighborhood communities. Programs are developed alongside a variety of partners with valuable perspectives – including the New York Economic Development Corporation, the program's NYCx Tech Leadership Advisory Council, various accelerator programs across the city including Company (formerly Grand Central Tech), and New Lab – with a focus to support diverse founders. Recently, the "Brownsville Co-Lab Challenge: Zero Waste in Shared Space" brought together startups and community residents in one of Brooklyn's more underserved neighborhoods to ideate and innovate around the idea of trash collection.

Extending tech solutions into neighborhoods that have traditionally been overlooked not only provides startups with hands-on experience but also recognizes that entrepreneurs come from everywhere inspires the next generation of New Yorkers to get involved in their communities and make public service a part of their mission. "The future of New York City is to really be the fairest big city in America," Jeremy says, "and technology and smart city technology are tools to support that vison so long as New Yorkers are a part of the problem-solving process."

WHERE NEXT?